ATLAS OF CURSED PLACES

ATLAS OF
CURSED
PLACES

*A Travel Guide
to Dangerous and Frightful
Destinations*

OLIVIER LE CARRER ✷ SIBYLLE LE CARRER

BLACK DOG
& LEVENTHAL
PUBLISHERS
NEW YORK

Black Dog & Leventhal Publishers
Hachette Book Group
1290 Avenue of the Americas
New York, NY 10104

www.blackdogandleventhal.com

Printed in Singapore

Cover design by Red Herring Design. Original interior design by Audrey Sednaoui and François Morenos, adapted by Red Herring Design.

IM

First Edition: October 2015
10 9 8 7 6 5 4 3 2 1

Black Dog & Leventhal Publishers is an imprint of Hachette Books, a division of Hachette Book Group. The Black Dog & Leventhal Publishers name and logo are trademarks of Hachette Book Group, Inc.

The Hachette Speakers Bureau provides a wide range of authors for speaking events. To find out more, go to www.HachetteSpeakersBureau.com or call (866) 376-6591.

The publisher is not responsible for websites (or their content) that are not owned by the publisher.

Library of Congress Cataloging-in-Publication Data available upon request.
ISBN: 978-1-6319-1000-5

CONTENTS

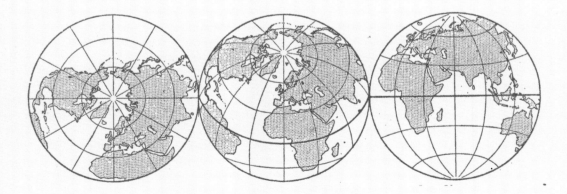

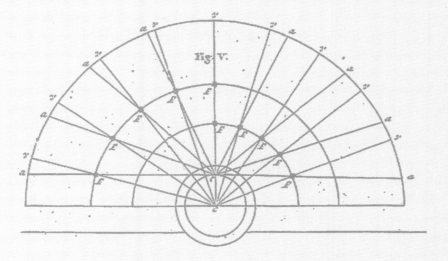

AMONG THE ISLANDS OF THE NEW WORLD

BENEATH THE ATLANTIC BREEZE

THE HAZARDS *of* TRAVELING

With regard to curses, mankind has had a close shave. The very first pages of the Bible give a pretty clear idea of the wretched atmosphere in which the world was created. In the book of Genesis, God, infuriated by Adam's disobedience, utters the words "Cursed is the ground for thy sake!" (3:17) and informs the first human that, instead of dwelling in the Garden of Eden, he will be compelled to tire himself out working an unproductive earth in order to survive. In what looks like a general curse on the heads of all future Earth-dwellers, Adam is spared no detail of the difficulties his new status will bring: "In sorrow shalt thou eat of it all the days of thy life; thorns also and thistles shall it bring forth to thee; and thou shalt eat the herb of the field; in the sweat of thy face shalt thou eat bread, till thou return unto the ground; for out of it wast thou taken" (3:17–19).

For many of Earth's seven billion human beings, vestiges of the Creator's initial fit of pique are still, to this day, all too visible. And by no means in every case is it because the land is low-lying or barren. Since the time of the Old Testament, humanity has found more effective ways of damning itself, coming up with bizarre town planning concepts and inventing all manner of jobs, one more disagreeable than the last—in mines, factories, industrial fishing, and call centers—in other words, devising an almost infinite number of hells that no god or demon would ever have dared to contemplate back in the day.

The cases described in this book are a reminder of how much the woes of a place owe to mankind's overactive imagination. The curses uttered by the prophets of the past, awe-inspiring as they might be, were always reassuringly abstract: Only those lacking the good sense to simply ignore them were bound.

Not all cursed places are the same. There are three main rationales for awarding this distinctly off-putting appelation. The classic one, the one closest to the original sense of the word, is of course bound up with admonitions of a mystical order. Particularly abundant from antiquity to the Middle Ages, it has to be said that this category is treading water today due to a lack of authors capable of reinvigorating the genre. However, the tradition is being maintained in certain regions thanks to the zeal of readers the good old sacred texts. Edifying examples of this tendency can be found in the Middle East.

In parallel with the decline of the religious strand, a preternatural variant has experienced undeniable success over the last two centuries. This is the supernatural or paranormal phenomenon, which is capable of unleashing the most dreadful events in peaceful backwaters that have done nothing to upset anyone. From the Bermuda Triangle to the Amityville house of horrors, these are the most fascinating cases, as they are open to the wildest interpretations.

The second category of cursed place invites less controversy but is even more daunting.

It consists of places that, for a variety of entirely natural reasons (appalling climate, proximity of an irascible volcano, colonies of unfriendly beasts, uncultivable land . . .), enduringly blight the lives of the local populations or present a real danger to local people and visitors alike.

The third, and no less daunting, category comprises locations that have been rendered uninhabitable by human activity. The causes may be varied (pollution, criminality, financial upheavals, insoluble border disputes . . .) but the results are virtually identical: hellish living conditions for the inhabitants—and, what's more, no real hope of change, the perenniality of the problem sadly being a key characteristic in this as in the other categories. It goes without saying that the three major categories of cursed place can also come together at the same site—to the enormous misfortune of all concerned.

Taking all the above into consideration, the reader may well wonder what virtue there is in concerning oneself with these unwelcoming places. The following pages will provide unsuspecting tourists with all the information they need to avoid being trapped in an impossible location by an unscrupulous tour operator. They also offer inquisitive souls a remarkable summary of the terrifying yet enthralling complexity of humanity, enabling them to draw the consoling conclusion that, although Everest and the moon may already have been conquered, many mysterious places remain to be explored and understood in the world below.

AT THE HEART OF OLD EUROPE

Château de Montségur

*

Rocca-Sparviera

*

Nuremberg

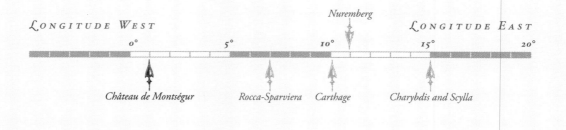
42°52′N – 1°49′E

CHÂTEAU DE MONTSÉGUR

SATAN'S SYNAGOGUE

Before turning their thoughts to the intriguing legends associated with these ruins, hikers should watch where they put their feet. The consequences could be disastrous for any clumsy person who strays off the marked footpaths and loses his or her footing on the edge of the precipices that drop away on every side of this aptly nicknamed "citadel in the sky." And let us not forget that early in 1244 it was a feat of rock climbing that sealed the fate of the Cathars when they were besieged here by the army of King Louis IX. After seven months, during which traditional military strategies had brought nothing but failure, Hugues des Arcis, the commander of the forces encamped at the foot of this eagle's nest, finally decided to send a small group of particularly agile soldiers up the cliff face. Under cover of darkness, this detachment reached the summit, captured a watchtower, and installed a trebuchet, with which it proceeded to bombard the interior of the castle without respite, making life impossible for the besieged, who were forced to surrender after a few weeks.

The fate of this community, the last bastion of the Cathar faith in France, is well known. One Sunday in March 1244, the day of the equinox, the believers—more than two hundred men and women—were led down to a pyre that had been set up at the foot of the hill, steadfastly refusing to renounce their faith. What else could they do, these pacifists who had taken a vow to show courage in the face of suffering and death? The name Cathar—from the Greek *katharos*, meaning "pure"—was given them by their contemporaries on account of their asceticism and refusal to compromise in any way. For the same reason, those who had undergone the rite of ordination called the *consolamentum* were known as *perfecti*, although among one another they preferred the terms "good man" and "good woman." The band of sympathizers protecting the pacifist Cathars were allowed to go free provided they pledged to stop supporting heresy and swore allegiance to the king of France.

The Château de Montségur that stands today is not the same fortress that existed at the time of these dreadful events. Historians, archeologists, and local storytellers cannot agree on all the details. For example, was the Cathars' place of martyrdom the *prats dels cremats* ("field of the burned"), as indicated today by a stele, or was it a neighboring hill? At this magnificent site, so many questions remain unanswered. There's the legendary Cathar treasure, said to have been held in safekeeping at Montségur before being

> *After seven hundred years the bay tree will flower again.*

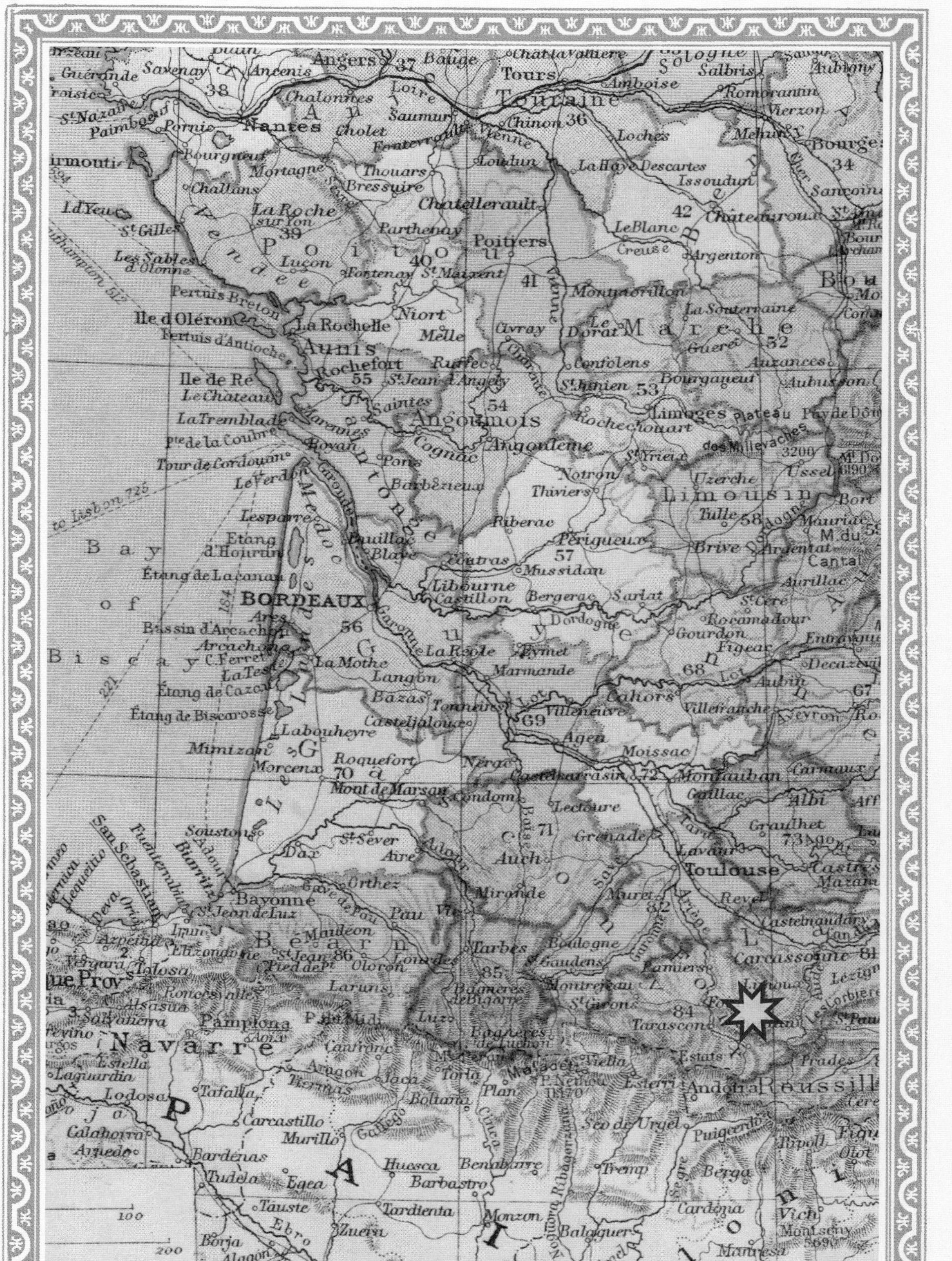
Angers
Baugé
Tours
Amboise
Salbris
Guérande
Savenay
Ancenis
Chalonnes
Loire
Touraine
Romorantin
Vierzon
St. Nazaire
Paimboeuf
Pornic
Nantes
Cholet
Saumur
Chinon 36
Loches
Bourges
Bourgneuf
Mortagne
Thouars
Loudun
La Haye Descartes
Issoudun
34
Challans
Bressuire
Chatellerault
I. d'Yeu
La Roche sur Yon
Parthenay
Poitiers
42
Chateauroux
St. Gilles
39
LeBlanc
Les Sables d'Olonne
Luçon
40
Fontenay
St. Maixent
41
Creuse
Argenton
Pertuis Breton
Montmorillon
Ile d'Oléron
La Rochelle
Niort
Melle
Civray
Le Dorat
Marche
La Souterraine
Pertuis d'Antioche
Aunis
Guéret
52
Rochefort
Ruffec
Confolens
Auzances
Ile de Ré
55
St. Jean d'Angely
St. Junien
53
Bourganeuf
Aubusson
Le Chateau
Saintes
54
Limoges
plateau
La Tremblade
Marennes
Angoumois
Rochechouart
Pte. de la Coubre
Royan
Cognac
Angoulême
des Millevaches
Tour de Cordouan
Pons
St. Yrieix
3200
Le Verdon
Barbezieux
Notron
Uzerche
Ussel
Thiviers
Limousin
to Lisbon 726
Lesparre
Riberac
Tulle
58
Mauriac
Etang d'Hourtin
Pauillac
Blaye
Perigueux
Brive
Argentat
Bay
57
Cantal
Étang de Lacanau
Coutras
Mussidan
Aurillac
Libourne
Castillon
Bergerac
Sarlat
of
BORDEAUX
St. Céré
Bassin d'Arcachon
56
Dordogne
Rocamadour
Arcachon
Gourdon
Biscay
C. Ferret
La Mothe
La Réole
Eymet
Figeac
Marmande
68
Lot
Langon
Decazeville
Étang de Cazau
Aubin
67
Bazas
Tonneins
Cahors
Villefranche
Étang de Biscarosse
Casteljaloux
69
Villeneuve
Aveyron
Labouheyre
Agen
Mimizan
Moissac
Roquefort
Nérac
Morcenx
70
Castelsarrasin
72
Montauban
Carmaux
Mont de Marsan
Condom
Gaillac
Albi
Lectoure
71
Graulhet
Soustons
St. Sever
Grenade
Lavaur
Dax
Aire
Auch
Toulouse
Castres
San Sebastian
Biarritz
Orthez
Mirande
Bayonne
Muret
Revel
St. Jean de Luz
Pau
82
Castelnaudary
Mauléon
Béarn
Tarbes
Boulogne
L
Carcassonne
St. Jean Pied de Port
86
Lourdes
Oloron
St. Gaudens
Pamiers
Tolosa
85
Montrejeau
Roncesvalles
Laruns
Bagnères de Bigorre
St. Girons
84
Alsasua
Pamplona
Luz
Tarascon
Navarre
Bagnères de Luchon
Estella
Aragon
Jaca
Estats
Prades
Laguardia
Andorra
Roussill
Lodosa
Tafalla
Boltaña
Plan
Esterri
Seo de Urgel
P
Carcastillo
Puigcerda
Ripoll
Olot
Calahorra
Murillo
Arnedo
Bardenas
Huesca
Benabarre
Tremp
Berga
Tudela
Egea
A
Barbastro
Tauste
Tardienta
Cardona
Vich
100
Ebro
Zuera
Monzon
Balaguer
Montseny
Borja
Alagon
Manresa
200
Steamer Routes
Saragosse
Lerida
Igualada
Los Monegros
Granollers

smuggled out to an unknown destination. And then there are the four men deputed by the community to slip away under the utmost secrecy prior to the ultimate surrender, carrying with them who knows what. Items of treasure? Precious documents? Mysterious keys enabling the Cathar tradition to be revived elsewhere? At Montségur nothing seems impossible. In the last century a team of German researchers came, with the blessing of the Nazi regime, to investigate, convinced that the castle housed the Holy Grail, the famous cup believed to have been used to catch Christ's blood.

What should we make of the site's architecture, of the spectacular alignment of the sun's rays at solstice time, as if its architects had wanted the castle to function as a kind of astronomical calendar? And doesn't its floor plan reflect the constellation of Boötes, with the donjon representing the star Arcturus? Is it also mere

The believers were led down to a pyre that had been set up at the foot of the hill.

chance that "Cant del Boièr" (Song of the Herdsman) remains one of the most popular folk songs in the Occitanian canon, with some people reading into its words a coded message addressed to future generations?

"After seven hundred years the bay tree will flower again"—and with it, no doubt, the Cathar faith. Thus were the words of the troubadour in the Occitania of old. Or was it the last of the perfecti to be burned at the stake? Or even a poet born generations later? Basically, nobody knows. It is even possible that the bay tree could be an olive tree, and that the date is regularly adjusted so that it never loses its relevance. No matter. The legend remains perplexing enough for visitors to be drawn in by its verses while contemplating the ruins of what the inquisitors called "Satan's synagogue"—but never quite managed to utterly destroy.

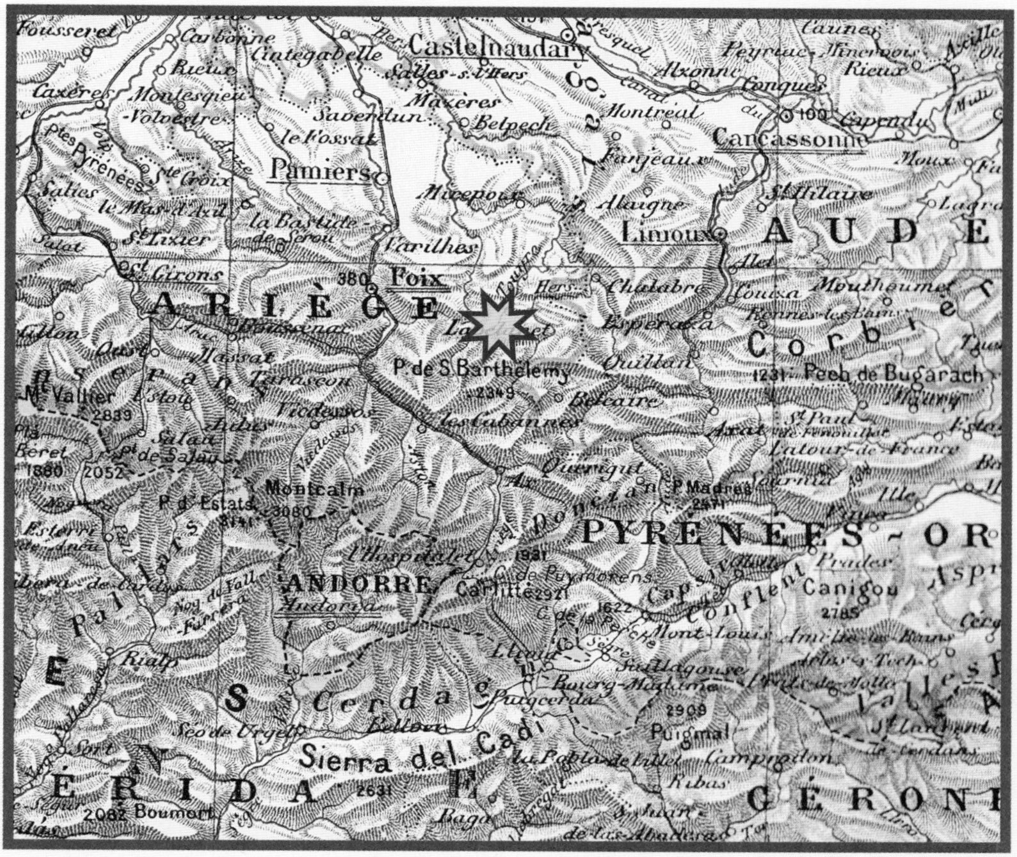

Fousseret
Carbonne
Cintegabelle
Castelnaudary
Salles-s-l'Hers
Mazères
Saverdun
Belpech
Alzonne
Conques
Montréal
Carcassonne
100
Capendu
Peyriac-Minervois
Caunes
Rieux
Montesquieu-Volvestre
Cazères
le Fossat
Pamiers
Mirepoix
Fanjeaux
Ste Croix
le Mas d'Azil
St Lizier
St Girons
la Bastide-de-Sérou
Varilhes
Limoux
AUDE
St Hilaire
Alet
Couiza
Mouthoumet
380
Foix
ARIÈGE
Chalabre
Esperaza
Quillan
Massat
Tarascon
P. de S. Barthélemy
2349
1231
Pech de Bugarach
Mt Vallier
2839
Vicdessos
Belcaire
Axat
1880
2052
Querigut
P. Madres
Montcalm
P. d'Estats
3080
PYRENEES
1931
ANDORRE
Andorra
Carlitte
2921
1622
Capsir
Conflent
Canigou
2785
Mont-Louis
Rialp
Saillagouse
Bourg-Madame
Puigcerda
2909
Puigmal
Seo de Urgel
Sierra del Cadi
Camprodon
Ribas
2631
2082 Boumort

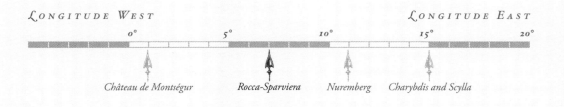
43°53´N – 7°17´N

ROCCA-SPARVIERA
THE PHANTOM VILLAGE

With its breathtaking panorama, the fame of Rocca-Sparviera (meaning "rock of the sparrow hawk") would no doubt be assured, even without the help of legend. But what evil spell could have been cast on this place to cause its inhabitants to desert such sublime views? Before abandoning this place, the local people had achieved the remarkable feat of constructing a bizarre village perched more than three thousand feet up a mountainside and an hour's walk along a steep path from the nearest hamlet. The second mystery—that of its origins— must remain unanswered: All that's known is that Rocca-Sparviera goes back to the twelfth century or before. A hundred years or so later the village is recorded as having a church and 150 parishioners. Had the castle already been built by then? Opinions differ, but a contract of infeudation in the name of a certain Pierre Marquesan, who acquired the fief for seven hundred gold florins, testifies to its existence the next century. The community grew year by year until it numbered some 350 souls.

And then, at the dawn of the fifteenth century, everything started to go wrong. A swarm of locusts devastated the modest crops, causing a famine that lasted several years. A diabolical succession of outbreaks of the plague, changes in alliance that threatened the security of the village, and the financial ruin of the lord of the manor were followed in 1564 by an earthquake that destroyed a number of houses. Subsequent tremors in 1612 and 1618 eventually laid the Rocca-Sparviera village to waste. In 1723, the village priest became the last diehard to abandon the ruins.

Were these entirely natural catastrophes? Evidently not, if one is to believe accounts of the awful Christmas Eve of 1357, when Queen Joanna of Naples was staying in Rocca-Sparviera as the guest of her vassal and decided to attend midnight mass at the neighboring village of Coaraze. Nothing in the life of Joanna, who was married at the age of eight, widowed at twenty, and remarried a further three times, ever went smoothly, so plentiful were her enemies both outside and inside her family. A shattering surprise greeted her upon her return: the sight of her two murdered children, their bodies displayed on the table as if the centerpiece of some macabre banquet. As she departed the following day, insane with grief and anger and having first set fire to the castle, she is supposed to have sworn that "No rooster or hen will ever crow again on this blood-soaked rock." Although the reality of Joanna's adventures in Provence casts some doubt over the chronology of the affair, the barrenness and instability of the mountain, which left has nothing but these sinister yet magnificent ruins, will ultimately have lent the legend an air of truth.

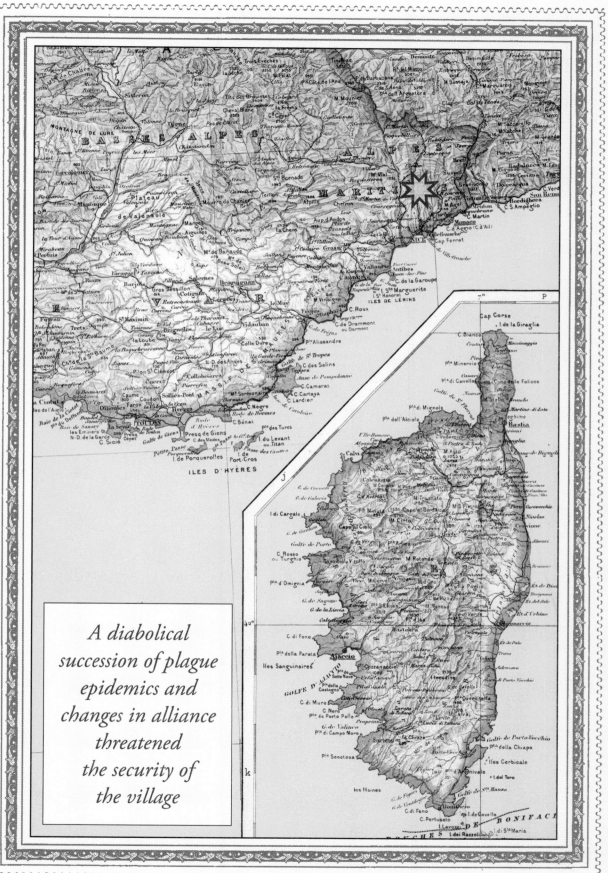

A diabolical
succession of plague
epidemics and
changes in alliance
threatened
the security of
the village

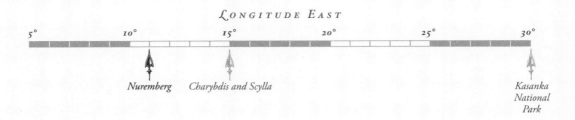
49°26′N – 11°4′E

NUREMBERG

THE SINISTER REVERBERATION OF MARCHING BOOTS

Every decade is a new dawn. In the flower-adorned streets of this ancient imperial city, visitors' thoughts rarely turn, after all this time, to the sound of boots that once reverberated here before extending their murderous din across the planet. In the twenty-first century, Nuremberg is on people's lips for infinitely more frivolous and respectable reasons: Every year in early February it hosts the Spielwarenmesse, the world's largest toy fair. After this the modern, air-conditioned pavilions of the Messezentrum welcome Feuer Trutz, a trade fair dedicated to fire prevention, should any proof be needed that the lessons of the past have been well and truly learned.

The majority of visitors strolling the exhibition center are no doubt unaware that they are walking on the exact spot where Nazi troops paraded in the 1930s, for this was the heart of the Reichsparteitagsgelände (literally, "Congress Area of the Reich Party," but more informally known as the Nazi Party Rally Grounds). This immense complex was dreamed up by Adolf Hitler's architect-builder Albert Speer as a venue for the annual rally and demonstrations of military strength of the National Socialist regime. With a little

The Führer had modestly predicted that nothing in the world would be able to remotely match its splendor.

application and a good historical map, the images easily take shape again. The impressive axis that extends for a little more than a mile in a northwesterly direction is the legendary Grosse Strasse, the monumental avenue leading from the Luitpoldarena, the assembly ground of the SA and SS, to the Märzfeld, the seven-hundred-hectare arena designed to accommodate several hundred thousand drilling soldiers. Between the two lay the imposing Roman-style amphitheater of the Kongresshalle and the interminable grandstand of the Zeppelinfeld, immortalized in so many photographs, with its military standards and lighting effects emphasizing the endless lines of uniforms, that it has become the very emblem of terrifying Nazi fervor.

Eighty years later, the loose slabs of the Grosse Strasse have been invaded by wild grasses, and the avenue leads nowhere. Preoccupied by other, more destructive tasks, Albert Speer never completed his equivalent of the Champ de Mars in Paris. Also unfinished is the Kongresshalle, which is still roofless today, a characterless pile whose first stone was laid at the very moment the so-called Nuremberg Laws, the first official anti-Semitic measures, were announced in 1935.

Holstein
Lübeck
Rostock
Greifswald
Wolgast
Demmin
Anklam
Swinemünde
Bützow
Wismar
Schwerin
Güstrow
Itzehoe
Glückstadt
Elmshorn
Ratzeburg
Altona
Wandsbek
HAMBURG
MECKLENBURG
Parchim
Karow
Waren
Malchin
Friedland
Neu Brandenburg
Neustrelitz
Prenzlau
Lehe
Bremerhaven
Geestemünde
Stade
Harburg
Lauenburg
Ludwigslust
Wilhelmshaven
Brake
Oldenburg
OLDEN-BURG
Delmenhorst
Bremen
Lüneburg
Lüneburg
Dömitz
Pritzwalk
Wittstock
Wittenberge
Neu Ruppin
Angermünde
Verden
Soltau
Ülzen
Cloppenburg
Hanover
Heath
Salzwedel
Oranienbg
Eberswalde
Quakenbrück
Diepholz
Nienburg
Celle
Stendal
Brand
Rathenow
Spandau
BERLIN
Osnabrück
Minden
Linden
Hanover
Öbisfelde
Charlottenbg
Köpenick
Bückeburg
Lehrte
Brunswick
Kalbörde
Brandenbg
Potsdam
Herford
Hildesheim
Helmstedt
Burg
burg
Luckenwalde
LIPPE
Bielefeld
Hameln
Wolfenbüttel
Magdeburg
Detmold
Goslar
Halberstadt
Zerbst
ANHALT
Jüterbog
Holzminden
Paderborn
Wernigerode
Stassfurt
Quedlinbg
Wittenberg
Dessau
Lippstadt
Soest
Warburg
Klausthal
Northeim
Aschersleben
Köthen
Bitterfeld
Torgau
Falkenberg
Finsterwalde
Göttingen
Eisleben
Saxony
Halle
Eilenburg
Elsterwerda
Arnsberg
Iserlohn
Arolsen
WALDECK
Münden
Nordhsn
Sondershsn
Sangerhausen
Merseburg
Wurzen
Cassel
Mühlhausen
LEIPZIG
Riesa
Grossenhain
Meissen
Barmen
Frankenbg
Eschwege
Naumburg
Weissenfels
Langensalza
Apolda
Zeitz
Döbeln
Hessen-
Erfurt
Altenbg
SAXONY
Eisenach
Gotha
Weimar
Jena
Freibg
Pirna
Hersfeld
Gera
Meerane
Chemnitz
Siegen
Marburg
THURINGIA
Glauchau
Zwickau
Wetzlar
Giessen
Schmalkalden
Rudolstadt
Saalfd
Greiz
Nassau
Fulda
Meiningen
Suhl
Schleitz
Reichenbach
Brüx
Limburg
Schlüchtern
Hildburghausen
Plauen
Komotau
Homburg
Friedberg
Coburg
Sonneberg
Ölsnitz
Taunus
Frankfurt
Kissingen
Hof
Saaz
Offenbach
Schweinfurt
Kulmbach
Karlsbad
Darmstadt
Aschaffenburg
CZECHO
Prague
Bayreuth
Eger
Marienbad
Würzburg
Bamberg
Worms
Odenwald
Kitzingen
Weinheim
Erlangen
Pilsen
Ludwigshafen
Mannheim
Fürth
Heidelberg
Speyer
Rothenbg
Nuremberg
Amberg
Künzelsau
Ansbach
Neumarkt
Karlsruhe
Heilbronn
Crailsheim
Gunzenhsn
BAVARIA
Pforzheim
Ludwigsbg
Ellwangen
Ratisbon (Regensburg)
Gmünd
Aalen
Nördlingen
Eichstätt
Straubing
Deggendorf
Stuttgart
Esslingen
Donauwörth
Göppingen
Heidenheim
Neuburg
Ingolstadt
WÜRTEMBERG
Tübingen
Blenheim
Landau
Dillingen
Pfaffenhofen
Passau
Ulm
Landshut
Augsburg
Freising
Mühldorf
Biberach
MUNICH
Hohenlinden
Landsberg
Wasserburg
Memmingen
Austri
Ravensburg
Rosenheim
Friedrichshafen
Kempten
Weilheim
Tölz

As for the megalomaniac Deutsches Stadion, this gigantic copy of the Panathenaic Stadium in Athens progressed no further than the earthworks. The Führer had modestly predicted that nothing in the world would be able to remotely match its splendor, with four hundred thousand seats, and that in the future all the Olympic Games would be held here, in the "most German of German cities." Today, at this spot the eye takes in not an imposing stadium but the down-at-the-heels caravans of an encampment of fairground people, the symbol of a site that was designed to impress the entire world but is now reduced to a sort of no-man's-land that everyone would rather forget. Hardly any tourists are seen loitering in this part of town; understandably they prefer strolling up and down the picturesque pedestrian lanes of the city center. By the River Pegnitz, which flows lethargically under a number of charming little stone bridges, the illusion is complete: Despite the hail of bombs, the old town looks like a picture-book illustration of the Middle Ages. Care is lavished on the house of the painter Albrecht Dürer, which is more than five hundred years old, and the city keeps a wary guard over its numerous museums and their contents, which include Martin Behaim's globe. Paradoxically, it is outside the walls of the old city that rare traces of the drama that unfurled last century can be detected: To the west, where the Justizpalast (Palace of Justice), the theatre in which between 1945 and 1946 the final act of the most bloody war in human history was played out, still stands; and, of course, to the southeast, on the unfinished building site of the Nazi Party Rally Grounds.

Thumbing its nose at the district's infernal past, the former SS barracks building, a few hundred yards from Grosse Strasse, now houses the High Commission for Refugees, demonstrating that one should never lose faith in mankind, even in the most cursed of places.

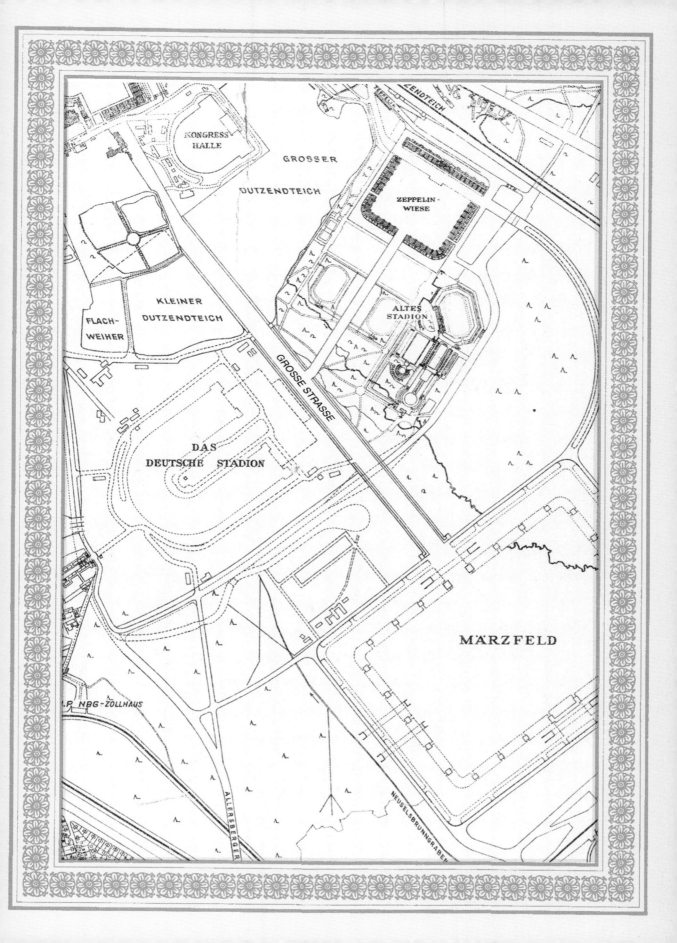

BETWEEN THE MEDITERRANEAN WORLD AND SOUTHERN AFRICA

The Tophet of Carthage

*

Oumaradi

*

Poveglia

*

Charybdis and Scylla

*

Kasanka National Park

*

Valley of the Kings

*

Gaza

*

Beirut

*

Moriah and Golgotha

*

Kibera

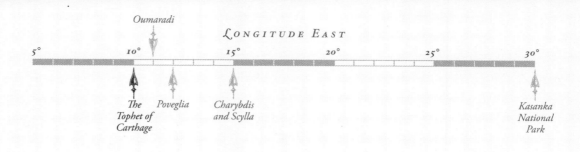

Oumaradi

LONGITUDE EAST

5° 10° 15° 20° 25° 30°

The
Tophet of
Carthage

Poveglia

Charybdis
and Scylla

Kasanka
National
Park

_36°50´N – 10°19´E_

THE TOPHET OF CARTHAGE

CHILDREN BURNED FOR THE GODS

The word _tophet_ alone is enough to spread unease. And if it has a number of meanings, well, they all strike fear in the heart. The biblical Tophet was a site outside Jerusalem in the hollow of the Valley of Hinnom where, three thousand years ago, the Canaanites burned children alive as offerings to their idols. The word was also used at that time to designate hell. And in a more technical though no less terrifying sense, it is also the term used throughout most of the Mediterranean basin to denote the actual pit in which human sacrifices were made. Notably in Carthage, whose _tophet_, known as the Salammbo, remains one of the most notorious. Twenty thousand funerary urns, mostly of very young children, have been discovered there by archaeologists. This is thought to be just a small portion of the remains buried in this necropolis quite unlike any other, because over the centuries urbanization has eaten away at the vestiges of antiquity and a good number of steles remain hidden beneath the gardens of the affluent villas that have sprung up here. The mythical city of Carthage, destroyed by the Romans in 146 B.C. and rebuilt a century later, has changed beyond recognition. In what has become an elegant suburb of Tunis, cypresses and bougainvillea lend the surroundings a certain charm, and the _tophet_ is notable only for its unobtrusiveness.

The place bears no resemblance to the way it looked in the first millennium B.C., when the Phoenicians who founded the city chose this insalubrious, marshy location as the site of the cult of Baal and Tanit. A strange place to worship deities? Not if one stops to consider the specifics of the religion, and in particular the fact that tens of thousands of children were burned here in an attempt by the city to win the gods' favor. The issue is so shocking that it remains hotly debated today, certain historians claiming that this was a "traditional" funerary installation where the only children to be cremated were stillborn babies. But most of the cremated infants were not newborn, and it is widely acknowledged that human sacrifice was practiced during the period in question.

Thus for six centuries the ashes of children accumulated within these precincts located at the foot of Byrsa Hill and a mere stone's throw from the ancient Punic ports. When space ran out, all that had to be done was to cover the site with a new layer of soil and continue, which explains why the stelae and urns can be found in several strata almost sixteen feet deep.

It is claimed that in order to satisfy the gods, each family had to sacrifice its firstborn male child. But their sacrifice did not do the city any good, as it was subsequently laid to waste and its population massacred, never again to play a part in world affairs. Is this the result of the curse supposedly uttered by the Romans at the time of the city's destruction, or is it because the earth of the _tophet_ was never able to digest all that blood?

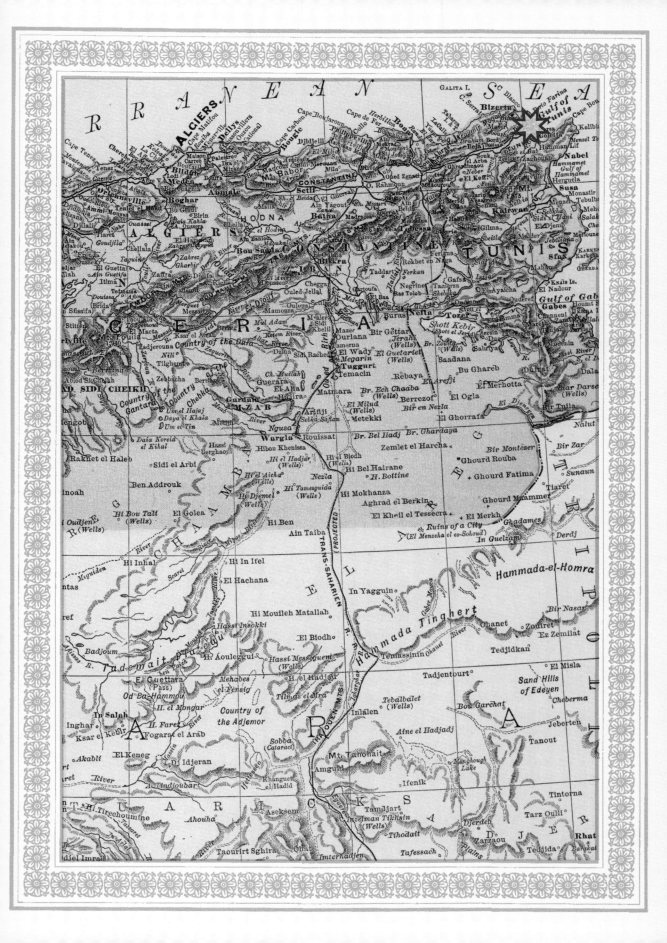

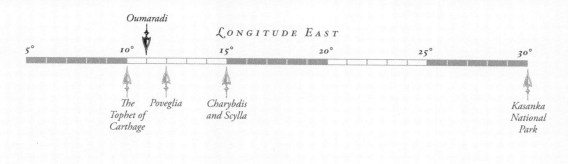

13°43´N – 11°12´E

OUMARADI
SHIPWRECKED BY SANDS

Here, the "doctor" is not always a wise counselor. This particular medic ravages entire villages and lays low their inhabitants. How the infernal Harmattan, the wind that blows across West Africa all winter long, came to acquire such a nickname is a mystery. Possibly because it makes the air of the blisteringly hot Sahel belt a little easier to breathe? In exchange for this somewhat minor benefit, it demands an exorbitant price. First there is an increased risk of illness as a result of ingesting the dust carried on the wind. Worse than this, however, is the progressive suffocation by sand of all human and plant life.

Forty years ago the Oumaradi villagers thought they had found the perfect site for a settlement, at least by the standards of the region: a small patch of forest, water, pastureland. And then the infernal cycle began. Successive droughts debilitated the vegetation that, until then, had stabilized the soil. The need for wood of a population that had grown in number over the years resulted in the clear-felling of trees, correspondingly reducing the degree of protection the copses afforded against the wind. Today, the houses are disappearing beneath the dunes, with only a few walls and dead treetops protruding from the sand. It is difficult to imagine that dozens of families once lived here. They have now rebuilt their homes a short distance away—provisionally, for who could hope to withstand the sand's insatiable appetite for long? The sand is driven by the wind, most often in the form of shifting, crescent-shaped dunes known as *barchans*, which are capable of consuming twenty feet of land per year. This may not sound like much, but it is enough to swallow up a village within a few years—without the inhabitants' shovels being able to do the slightest thing about it. The wind frays the forward-facing horns of the *barchan* while pushing the sand toward the crest of the dune. As soon as the ridge starts to lean over too perilously, the excess tumbles forward. And so the crushing waves advance unstoppably, swallowing whatever trees, crops, and homes lie in its path.

The Harmattan is not always solely to blame for the disaster. The coup de grâce sometimes comes from the southwest, with the humid monsoon wind that drives other dunes back up from an unexpected direction, as if to attack mankind's derisory defenses from the rear.

Oumaradi has disappeared without trace. And other villages, both in Nigerian territory and in the neighboring countries, are also on the verge of disappearing, struck by the same scourge. No measures to combat the sands will be effective unless the sky decides to deliver a little more rain.

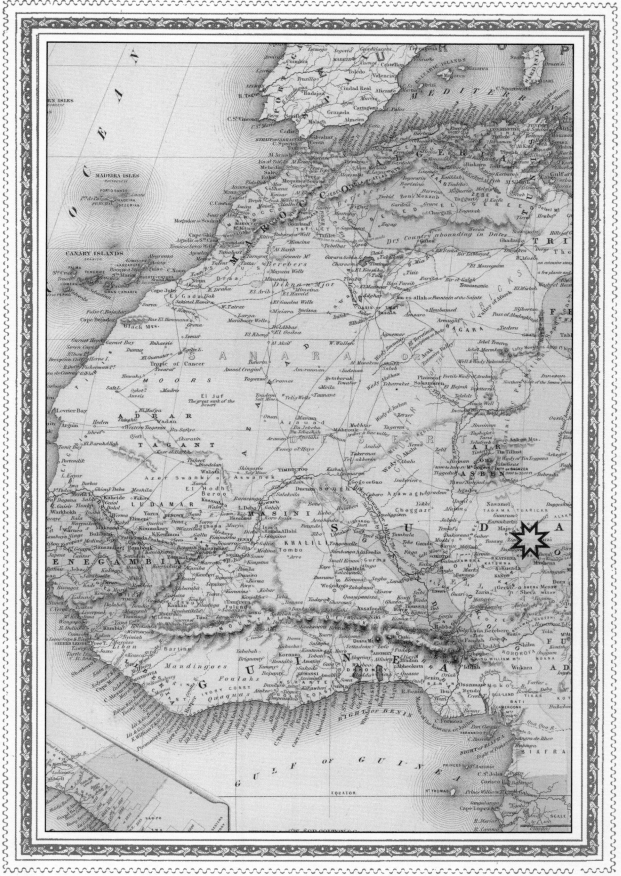

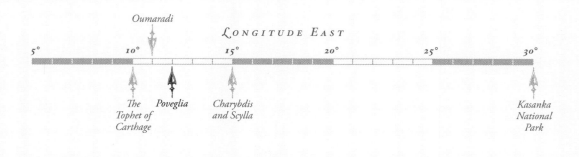

Oumaradi

LONGITUDE EAST

5°   10°   15°   20°   25°   30°

The
Tophet of
Carthage

Poveglia

*Charybdis
and Scylla*

*Kasanka
National
Park*

45°22′N – 12°19′E

POVEGLIA

THE ISLAND OF DEATH

In Veneto it is said that when a bad man dies, he wakes up on Poveglia. At first glance, this refuge of the damned, a small island located a few hundred meters from the Lido, looks perfectly pleasant: a blanket of green from which a large building overlooked by a charming bell tower emerges. In other words, it is altogether more appealing than the soulless buildings that front the sandbar across the water.

As one approaches the island, this initial impression changes completely and a sense of unease sets in. The roofs have collapsed, the windows have been ripped out, the walls are cracked, and the whole structure is being overtaken by rampant vegetation. How can such a place, just ten minutes by boat from the splendors of the Serenissima, a corner of the earth that until the fourteenth century accommodated several hundred families, produced salt and a much-enjoyed wine, and indeed flourished to such an extent that for a while it had its own autonomous government, simply have been abandoned?

As a symbol of its disgrace, Poveglia now enjoys the dubious distinction of being the only place in the Venetian Lagoon not served by public transport. The *vaporetto* from San Zaccaria to Chioggia (line 19) is happy to contribute to the steady erosion of the island's shoreline without ever stopping there. Although Poveglia may be little visited, it is much spoken of. Indeed, talk of this island has spread beyond the borders of Europe and it now enjoys a reputation as one of the most haunted places on the planet thanks to the 160,000 bodies believed to be buried in these few acres of ground to which, over the centuries, victims of the plague and lepers were deported and where a psychiatric hospital and then an old age home were later built. It is said that the souls of the plague-stricken roam the island in such large numbers that they have disturbed the minds of the living, notably the onetime director of the hospital, who is said to have been subject to bouts of madness that led him to conduct dubious experiments on—and bump off—numbers of his patients, and eventually to commit suicide by throwing himself from the *campanile*.

The archives of the municipality of Venice,

> *The souls of the plague-stricken roam the island in such large numbers that they have disturbed the minds of the living.*

however, are more tight-lipped than the legend. They offer no evidence of any enforced exile of either Black Death or leprosy sufferers to Poveglia. Might not the rumor mill have confused Poveglia with another islet, known as Lazzaretto Vecchio, which played a similar role in days gone by? And neither do the records shed any light on the opening of a psychiatric hospital on the island. They simply record dryly that in the eighteenth century the island passed into the control of the health authorities, who used it as a quarantine station for boats arriving from the open sea before they received permission to moor in Venice itself. It then accommodated a care and rest home for former members of Venetian crews before eventually, in the twentieth century, welcoming retired folk from all walks of life. Nowhere can any mention be found of a mad doctor. The center closed in 1968, after which time it received only the occasional visit from wine growers who came to tend the vines. The only verifiable drama in the island's history is its utter abandonment. However, not everyone will be convinced by the dry facts presented by the official documents, not when legend tells such a different story.

Perlan

Mestre

Campalto ○ C. Oselino

C. Oselino

B u r a ...

Batt.

Batt.

Batt. S. 6

L a n g o o

Fort Marghera

Railway Br.

Murano

S. Michel

Barbaioga

F^t S. Secondo

Batt.

S. 6

VENICE
(Venezia)

S. Elei

C. Brenta

S. Giorgio
in Alga

La Grazia ○ S. Servolo

Fusina

S. Angelo

S. Clemente Lazaro

S.
Lazaro ○

Old Lazaretto

S. Spirito ○

Batt. ...

M a l a m o c c o

Malamocc

Batt.

Fortino

Poveglia
Batt.

L a g o o n

Malamocc

Batt.

Campana
Bastion

Fisol.

C. Piovego

Bastion

Fort Alberoni

Litorale di

Cornio ○

Porto di Malam

Bastion

Fort S. Pietro

L A G O O N

Spignon Ch.

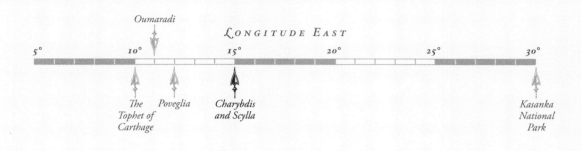

Oumaradi

LONGITUDE EAST

5°   10°   15°   20°   25°   30°

The
Tophet of
Carthage

Poveglia

Charybdis
and Scylla

Kasanka
National
Park

38°13′N – 15°36′E

CHARYBDIS AND SCYLLA
A HIGH-RISK CRUISE

The good thing about millennia-old legends is that we no longer really feel threatened by their horrors. Rarely will any sensible sailor navigating the Strait of Messina think that the terrifying monster Scylla is waiting around the next promontory to devour his crew. And even if he's worried about Homer's hidden metaphorical meanings (isn't Scylla merely a dangerous reef lying in wait to destroy his frail vessel?), a good nautical chart will generally provide ample reassurance of a safe route.

On the other hand, he would be well advised to pay attention to the excesses of Charybdis, the insatiable daughter of Poseidon, for whom time has really been dragging since Zeus sent her into exile beneath the waves for a notorious act of insubordination. Having found no other way to relieve her boredom than to scare travelers out of their wits, she has the sea frequently conjure up whirlpools, or *garofali* as they are called hereabouts.

Mariners from the north claim that the local currents do not compare with Scandinavian maelstroms. This is a grave error, for this stretch of the Mediterranean is anything but the wide, peaceful river it appears to be; it is the plaything

But is this narrow sound really Homer's lair of the two monsters?

of two antagonistic bodies of water, the Tyrrhenian and Ionian seas. The *garofali* are adept at deceiving their public, lulling sailors into a false sense of security before flitting without warning to the other side of the strait. During the north-flowing current, Charybdis wavers between the lighthouse beach on the Sicilian shore and the mainland, close to the aptly named present-day port of Scilla, where she whips the sea into a fury. When the current is pushing southward, it is off the Punta Raineri, just before Messina, that she endangers small craft. It is also advisable to take into account the curious waves known as *tagli*, which come along and tease the *garofali* on their home ground, and the *bastardi*, the countercurrents that skirt the sheer walls of the strait, complicating the situation even further. And then of course there's the wind, throttled between the mountainsides and gathering more and more speed until it is capable of wreaking even greater havoc on the water.

In spite of all the technological progress that has been made in the meantime, the experience of being tossed from Charybdis to Scylla—or, if you prefer, caught between a rock and a hard place—is hardly any more comfortable than it

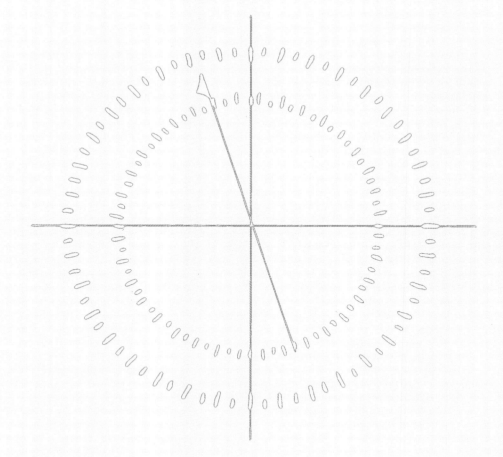

was in the time of Ulysses. But is this narrow sound really Homer's lair of the two monsters? The Strait of Gibraltar and the Bosporus have also, in turns, been suggested as the theater of Ulysses's misadventures. A number of historians are even convinced that contrary to the official theory, whereby Ulysses visited the entire Mediterranean basin, our hero never actually left Greek waters and that these two calamities were waiting for him a mere stone's throw from the island of Ithaca.

Today's sailors rarely dabble in archeology and comparative literature, but they are nevertheless well aware that the voyage to Messina is by no means always a piece of cake. And it now presents a new danger completely unknown three thousand years ago: the impressive volume of ferry traffic between Sicily and Calabria, which is capable of giving even the most serene of captains a gray hair or two.

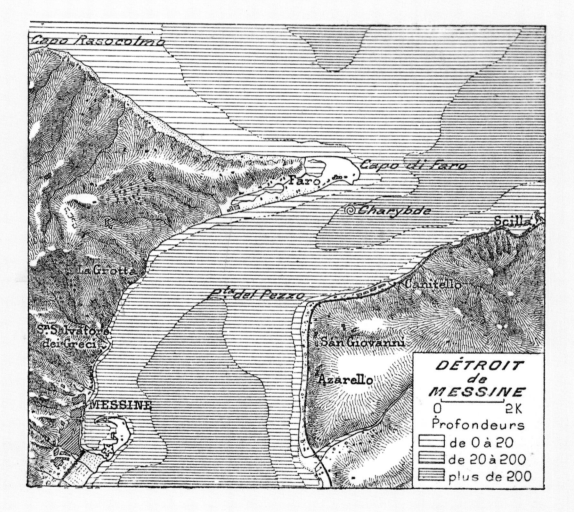

Capo Rasocolmo

Capo di Faro

Faro

Charybde

Scilla

La Grotta

p.ta del Pezzo

Canitello

c.a S.lvatore
dei Greci

San Giovanni

Azarello

MESSINE

DÉTROIT
de
MESSINE

0   2K

Profondeurs

de 0 à 20

de 20 à 200

plus de 200

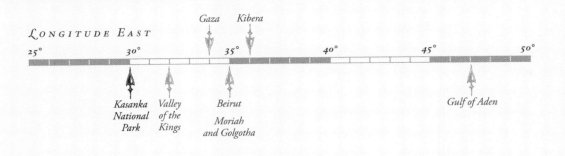

LONGITUDE EAST

25° 30° Gaza 35° Kibera 40° 45° 50°

Kasanka
National
Park

Valley
of the
Kings

Beirut

Moriah
and Golgotha

Gulf of Aden

23°33′S – 30°05′E

KASANKA NATIONAL PARK
THE INVASION OF THE BATS

At first glance, this game park in Zambia, as one of the smallest reserves in the country and indeed in the whole of Africa, seemed predestined to remain under the radar. Devastated by poaching, it might even have folded in the 1980s had it not been for the British expatriate David Lloyd, who developed a passion for the place and devoted all his energy to its rehabilitation. Aided by the people of Serenje District and the Zambian authorities, he succeeded in reintroducing hippopotamus, antelope, elephant, and hundreds of species of birds, some of them extremely rare. But he couldn't have predicted that Kasanka's international fame would eventually rest on some other creatures that had not been invited to the party.

The best way to imagine the phenomenon that struck Kasanka National Park is to think of it as the African remake of one of Alfred Hitchcock's most unsettling films, only with bats—millions of them that arrived from who knows where—instead of birds. Every year during the dying days of October, at the very beginning of the rainy season, millions of these small creatures swoop down on the forest of Fibwe at the heart of the park and take off again in December for an unknown destination. It is considered the world's largest mammal migration. Attempts to track them by means of small transmitters have not yielded any answers up to now, because the flight recorders have fallen silent for no apparent reason after a mere few hundred miles of flight.

For a period of almost two months, at dusk the sky above Kasanka regularly turns black as a result of the taking to flight of more than five million flying mammals over only two and a half acres. To see them up close is a truly impressive sight. This African species of bat—*Eidolon helvum*, also known as the straw-colored fruit bat—is somewhat forbidding, with an incredible little dog's head and sharp fangs. The invaders' main victims are the fruit trees: 330,000 tons of fruit disappear every year during the course of the raid.

The arrival of the fruit bats also encourages an influx of invariably ill-intentioned visitors. Excited by the promise of tender meat, crocodiles, pythons, and birds of prey crowd around the trees at Fibwe, on the lookout for a wrong move or the fall of a branch overladen with bats. Could these initially unwanted local predators unknowingly make the park's fortune by drawing in tourists?

Lake Rudolf
Wadelai
U G A N D A
Albert
Aruwimi
Unyoro
Wruli
Kioga L.
Jinja
Usoga
Elgon
Ruwenzori
L. Edward
Budu
Victoria Nyanza
Kenia
Tana
Kikuyu
Ukamba
Nairobi
Lowa
L. Kivu
C O N G O
B R I T I S H
Kilimanjaro
Taveta
Uzinja
Unyamwezi
Urambo
Nyangwe
Ujiji
Tabora
Lukuga
E A S T   A F R I C A
Albertville
Mpala
Karema
Usagara
Mpwapwa
Rikwa
Abercorn
Langenburg
Kazembe
Bukama
Bunkeya
Karonga
L. Bangweolo
Katanga
Elisabethville
Chitembo
Kota Kota
Nyasa
St Jameson
Broken Hill
Livingstonia
Zumbo
Zomba
Tete
Blantyre
Chiromo
Kafue
Mashonald
Salisbury
Charter
Sena
Chinde
Matabele Land
Manica
Victoria
Beira
Sofala
Bulawayo
Zimbabwe
Tuli
Limpopo
Gaza Land
Serowe
Shoshong
Pietersburg
Inhambane
Corrientes
P O R T U G U E S E   E A S T   A F R I C A
Transvaal
Pretoria
Johannesburg
Middelburg
Barberton
Swazi Ld
Lorenço Marquez
Delagoa B.
Tonga
St Lucia B.
Orange Free State
Bloemfontein
Basuto Ld
Natal
Zululd
Durban
Pietermaritzburg
Kokstad
Pondo Ld.
Tembu Ld.
Good Hope
K. Williamstown
East London
Grahamstown
Algoa B.
Elizabeth
Logh
Shidle
Bardera
Geledi
el Adhale
Mukdisho
Merka
Barawa
Jub
Kisimayu
Lamu
Witu
Malindi & Sabaki R.
Mombasa
Wanga
Pemba
Pangani
Zanzibar
Bagamoyo
Dar es Salaam
Rufiji
Mafia
Kilwa
Lindi
Masasi
Aldabra I. (Fr.)
C. Delgado
Rovuma
Ibo
Gt Comoro
Comoro Is. (Fr.)
Mohilla
Johanna
Mayotta
Nossi Be
P. Amelia
Luli
Mozambique
Majunga
C. St Andrew
Mozambique Chan.
Kilimane
Zambesi
Tamatave
Antananarivo
Andovoro
M A D A G A S C A R
Morondava
Manja
Fianarantsoa
Masindrano
Ambalo
Tullear
C. St Mary
To Tamatave 1363
To Mauritius 1532
To Melbourne
I N D

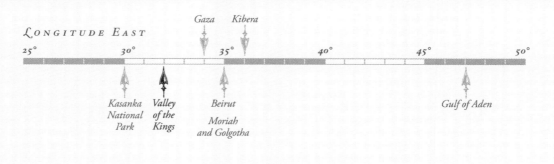

25°44´N – 32°36´E

VALLEY OF THE KINGS
THE CURSE OF ATEN

There are few more radiant settings than this simple necropolis, where the ocher of the rocks, warmed by a scorching sun, contrasts strikingly with the pale blue of a cloudless sky. Here the great and the good of Egypt are installed for all eternity in their majestic Valley of the Kings— an eternity alas all too theoretical given the zeal of both looters and archaeologists, to say nothing of the enthusiasm of the tourists.

Among all the pharaohs buried here, a mere stone's throw from the pomp of yesterday's Thebes and the air-conditioned hotels of today's Luxor, one in particular bears consideration for the indignities he has suffered. Under the official numbering system, which catalogs sixty-four burial places (twenty-seven of which are royal), he is known as Kings' Valley 62 (KV62) but more commonly as King Tutankhamun— or, to be precise, the *former* occupant, because luckless Tutankhamun, in common with a number of his predecessors and successors, was unceremoniously dislodged from his small but richly furnished underground vault and transferred to a glass case in the Egyptian Museum in Cairo, where the process of decay has been suspended. What a sad ending for this ruler who was judged by history as being of only minor significance but became famous in spite of himself. In life as in death, the evil eye has never left him. It is as if he were being made

to forever atone for the mistakes of his father, Amenhotep IV, alias Akhenaten, who was guilty of trying to replace the religion of the ancients with the cult of the sun disk Aten.

Born of the incestuous union between the heretical pharaoh and one of his sisters, the young Tutankhaten, as he was named at birth, would suffer throughout his life from a number of handicaps from which the practice of in-breeding—common during the New Kingdom— was clearly a factor. Having for some time been jointly groomed for accession to the throne along with his half sister Meritaten, he became pharaoh at nine years of age and was quickly married to one of his other half sisters, Ankhesenpaaten. This was an unhappy marriage, in terms of progeny at least, as the couple's two children were both stillborn. On the advice of his counselors, the king undertook to restore the cult of Amun, the ubiquitous god of ancient Egypt, and adopted the name Tutankhamun ("the living image of Amun"), although posterity was to give him little credit for this return to tradition. When he died in 1327 B.C., in all likelihood of an infection related to malaria, his name continued to be associated with his father's sun worship, in consequence of which all traces of his reign were systematically erased.

Three thousand years later, the pharaoh achieved phenomenal posthumous glory thanks to the perseverance of an English Egyptologist.

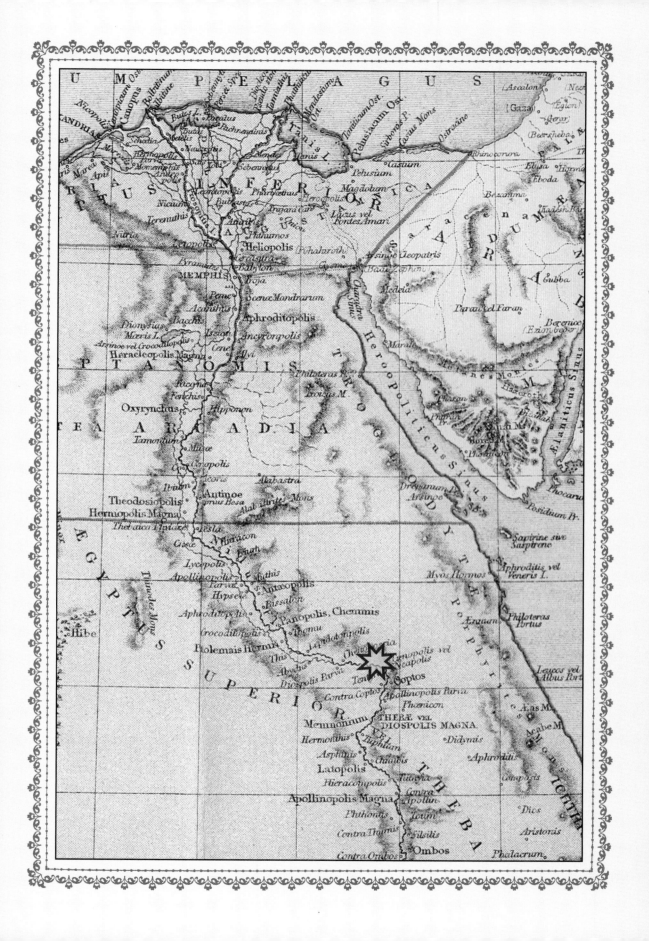

After thirty years of conducting excavations in most of the Egyptian necropolises, Howard Carter achieved his greatest triumph with this miraculous find. Unlike all its neighbors, which had been vandalized and emptied of their riches and even mummies, KV62 was virtually intact. The whole world succumbed to the charms of Tutankhamun's golden mask and discovered the splendors of a royal tomb in which nothing, or almost nothing, seemed to have been disturbed.

The public was also transfixed by the reporting of the curse that was said to plague anyone who disturbed a tomb. As Tutankhamun's tomb was being opened, the *New York Times* reported that a cobra found in Carter's home had killed his pet canary, which "made an impression on the native staff, who regarded it as a warning from the departed King against further intrusion on the privacy of his tomb." First to die four months later was Lord Carnarvon, Carter's backer, from a simple mosquito bite, followed by the deaths of some of Carnarvon's nearest and dearest, Carter's friends, and various archaeologists who had worked on the site. And let's not forget the suicide of Hugh Evelyn-White, one of the very first people to have entered the tomb. In total,

In total, twenty-seven suspicious deaths were recorded during the ensuing years.

twenty-seven suspicious deaths were recorded during the ensuing years. And what was to be made, several decades later, of the cerebral hemorrhage that struck down the Cairo-born director of antiquities immediately after signing the document authorizing the transportation of Tutankhamun's treasure to France for an exhibition at the Petit Palais in Paris? The press, aided and abetted by that fanatic of spiritualism Arthur Conan Doyle, had a field day with the curse. Doyle's fellow author Agatha Christie, meanwhile, took a resolutely pragmatic view of the affair, simply drawing upon the supposed curse for material for a new adventure featuring Hercule Poirot.

Perhaps the real curse of the Valley of the Kings lies elsewhere: in the inexorable deterioration of this unique site visited each day by six thousand tourists whose backpacks rub up against frescoes several thousand years old, who saturate the atmosphere of these long-shut-up vaults with their sweat and breath, and who defy the regulations by flashing away at these innocent relics from the past with their cameras. Presumably the curse will end only when peace has been restored to KV62 and the other burial chambers.

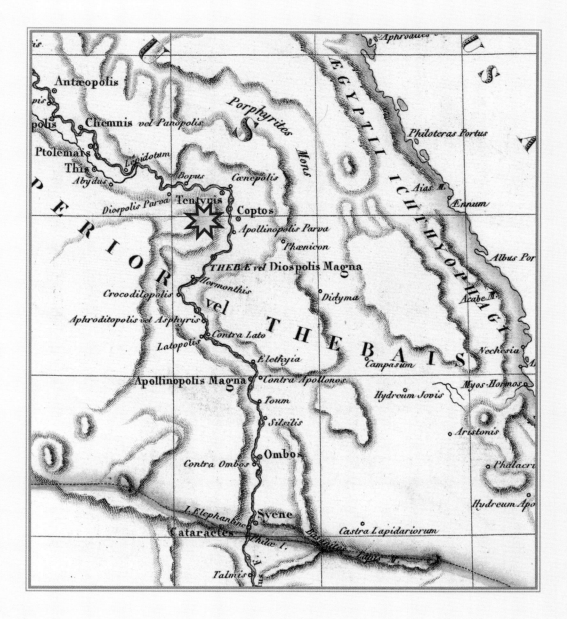

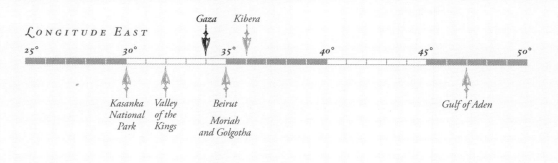

LONGITUDE EAST

25°   30°   35°   40°   45°   50°

Gaza   Kibera

Kasanka
National
Park

Valley
of the
Kings

Beirut

Moriah
and Golgotha

Gulf of Aden

31°31′N – 34°27′N

GAZA

A TERRITORY ADRIFT

History's sense of humor can be in dubious taste. How otherwise could it have transformed the four-letter word *Gaza*—a word that resembled nothing so much as *gauze*, the light fabric that has assuaged countless wounds, and indeed owes its name to the city of Gaza, which was a pioneer in its production—into a universal symbol of apparently incurable adversity? It must have so many stories to tell, this place, so many pictures to show other than ruins, wretched camps, the din of arms, and the fences within which it has been imprisoned by impenetrable geopolitical subtleties.

Before the era of unfinished cinderblock walls topped with sheet metal roofs, this place boasted magnificent edifices of stone—theaters, temples, monasteries, and mosques—and a prosperity and dynamism whose fame spread far beyond the borders of Palestine. Even the mythical city of Jerusalem was little more than a village compared to the scale and vitality of Gaza in days gone by!

In 1500 B.C., the Egyptians established an administrative base here from which to govern their possessions in the land of Canaan. The Philistines, a seafaring people originally from Crete, replaced the Egyptians three centuries later and were not content merely to bestow a new name—Palestine—on the region, but instead transformed Maiumas and then Anthedon (Gaza's seaports, the city itself being at that time perched on a hilltop two kilometers away from the sea) into essential ports of call for the entire eastern Mediterranean. Vast quantities of precious stones, perfumes, gold, spices, and, of course, slaves changed hands on their docks and in the local *caravanserais*. It is even claimed that the roads smelled of frankincense, so important was the trade in this aromatic resin transported from the southern Arabian Peninsula.

As the various powers waxed and waned, Gaza was passed from hand to hand, becoming in turn Assyrian, Babylonian, Persian, Greek, and then Roman. Although the development of the newly founded Alexandria cast a certain shadow over the city, at the dawn of the Christian era, Gaza was still an important center. Under Emperor Hadrian, it was praised for its school of rhetoric, its vast hippodrome, and not least for the excellent wine produced on the local slopes, which was exported to every corner of the empire. Trade prospered, but this didn't prevent rulers and religions from succeeding one another in turn. Marnas, the deity inherited from the Philistines, was eventually abandoned in favor of Christ. Churches and monasteries soared heavenward during the Byzantine era, and then came the turn of the mosque. For a while the Muslims were forced to defend their territory against the Crusaders, but then one after another the Mamluks, Ottomans, Egyptians,

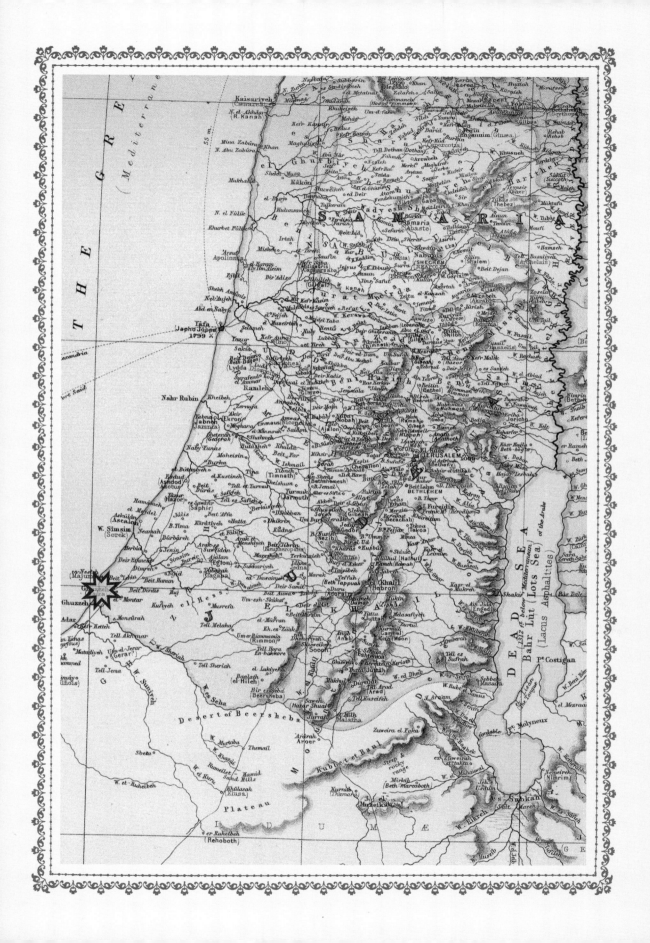

and English took control, for better or for worse, until the middle of last century.

The economic prosperity of old nevertheless conceals a cruel and frustrating reality: The city's main asset was at the same time its curse. Its position as a crossroads on the maritime and land routes between Africa and Asia Minor may look like a gift from God. As the epicenter of tensions between the local empires, however, it proved catastrophic. Ever since ancient times, religious conflict and changes of overlord have rarely been accompanied by civilized behavior, and the city's populations have, at various times, paid a heavy price.

It is the same story today, only with fewer old stones, a far bigger population, and an absence of gold and frankincense. The settlement is generally referred to now as Gaza City in order to distinguish the city proper from the territory with which it has become associated, the famous "strip" of the same name, a zone with unnatural boundaries measuring some forty by ten kilometers, whose population has increased twentyfold in just over sixty years as the result of a mass exodus from the neighboring slopes for reasons with which everyone is familiar. Thus there are now 1.6 million Gazans trapped in this geopolitical area still lacking any formal status. With 4,567 inhabitants per square kilometer, the Gaza Strip is one of the world's most densely populated places.

As the epicenter of tensions between the local empires, however, it proved catastrophic.

There is no relief in the water. In Gaza, Israeli coast guard patrols, no doubt eager to spare coastal dwellers the vicissitudes of the open sea, prohibit anyone from venturing more than three nautical miles (a little more than five kilometers) from the beach. This might be for the best as the sewers discharge straight into the Mediterranean, with the result that the fish caught along these coasts can have a rather peculiar taste.

The Gazans have also been preserved from the ups and downs of air travel ever since the runway of Yasser Arafat International Airport—a facility financed by the international community—was systematically plowed up by Israeli bulldozers barely three years after its inauguration by Bill Clinton. It is certainly true that there is a shortage of agricultural land in this enclave, which was once the larder of Palestine but no longer has enough space to feed all its people. Nor enough water. Thanks to the destruction of water pipes, out-of-order purification facilities, the impossibility of developing or even maintaining desalination plants, and pollution of various kinds, in the future there may be no water to drink.

In the meantime, life goes on. The economy functions after a fashion, and some projects actually are realized—a reminder, should one be needed, that the local people know how to build things other than refugee camps and homemade rockets.

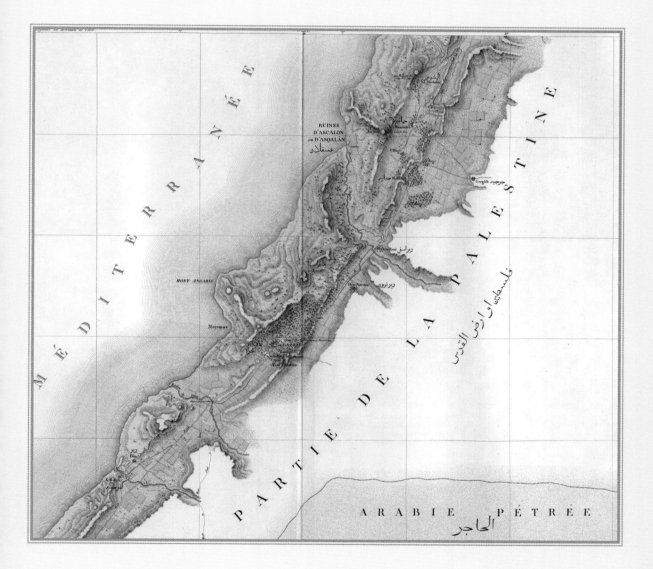

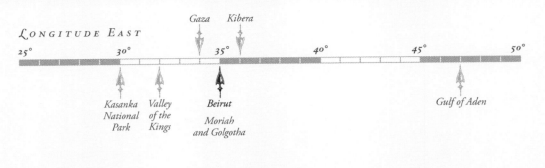

LONGITUDE EAST

25°   30°   35°   40°   45°   50°

Gaza   Kibera

Kasanka   Valley   Beirut   Gulf of Aden
National   of the
Park   Kings   Moriah
        and Golgotha

33°53′N – 35°30′E

BEIRUT

DESTRUCTION AND CONSTRUCTION

As building progresses, the war continues. Or vice versa. It is difficult to be sure in this city, which resembles nothing so much as a bewildering construction site in which one constantly wonders whether the clatter of machinery employed in public works might be replaced at any minute by that of gunfire. Beirut is a kind of urban metaphor for chaos, a permanent paradox in which ruined buildings, their walls still scarred by bullet and shell holes, stand face-to-face with the ultramodern glass towers that are springing up in a state of absolute anarchy more or less all over the place. A few minutes' walk along narrow alleys and broad avenues offers an insight into the complexity of the local situation. At the center of the West Beirut district of Bachoura, whose old dwellings have been eviscerated by the fighting but continue to house the odd family here and there, the past is still very much a part of the present. Six hundred feet farther on, you'll find yourself in another world in which the old Beirut has vanished and been replaced by rows of hip Western-style cafés and chic boutiques: the perfect embodiment of the worst clichés surrounding the local appetite for frivolity and luxury. As if the city hasn't already experienced enough misfortune, an attempt is being made to sweep away its heritage and start again—not so much for ideological or strategic reasons but for the sake of commerce and speculation.

In theory, at least, the conflicts are over. The civil war that began in 1975 (eventually claiming almost 200,000 victims, for the most part civilian) officially ended in 1990, and the July War of 2006, which left 1,600 dead as the result of clashes between Israeli soldiers and Hezbollah militia, is now regarded as ancient history. However, the word *peace* does not have the same meaning here that it has elsewhere. Only foreigners are surprised to see armed men patrolling the city, and bloody skirmishes between rival factions are an everyday occurrence—on days when there is no outright bombarding of one district by another, that is.

The malevolent European fairies who oversaw the birth of Lebanon in 1920, and subsequently its independence in 1943, transformed the land into a powder keg subject to outside influence and apt to explode at any moment. It is one of the few countries in the world in which parliamentary seats are apportioned according to religious affiliation, in which two rival governments can be in force at the same time, and in which the community militias are able to hold their own against the regular army. For the time being, as it approaches its centennial year, construction continues in the "white" country (from the Arabic *lubnān*, referring to the snow-covered Mount Lebanon) as in the capital . . . but for how long?

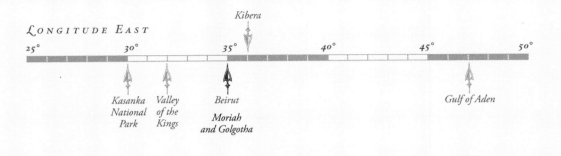

LONGITUDE EAST

25°   30°   35°   40°   45°   50°

Kibera

Kasanka
National
Park

Valley
of the
Kings

Beirut

Moriah
and Golgotha

Gulf of Aden

31°46′N – 35°13′E

MORIAH AND GOLGOTHA
SPIRITUAL NIGHTMARES

An honest pilgrim might be surprised to find included in a list of disturbing places these few hectares of holy land. Or even "thrice holy," to borrow a time-honored expression, as they are revered by Jews, Christians, and Muslims alike. The curse on these places relates not to the stories from the Torah, the New Testament, and the Qur'an, but rather to the somewhat excessive attachment of a sizeable proportion of their readers to these hills in Jerusalem.

Mount Moriah's and Mount Golgotha's respective histories both begin tragically before turning out well on the whole. The first is identified by some with the famous Temple Mount and is supposedly the setting for what is traditionally known as the "binding of Isaac," the moment when Abraham prepares to sacrifice his own son in observance of the divine commandment. Fortunately for the potential murderer and his victim, an angel stays Abraham's hand at the last moment. It was clearly a test of Abraham's faith. Isaac comes through it safe and sound, unlike the exegetes perhaps, who have had their work cut out over the centuries in interpreting this harrowing episode—in occasionally contradictory ways. A little farther to the west, Golgotha was renowned as the site of the crucifixion of Christ, followed by his resurrection.

The two hills may be only less than a half a mile apart, but they had very different fates. Located outside the walls of Jerusalem at the time of Christ, Golgotha was, over the course of the centuries, absorbed into the city; the current course of the city walls, erected less than five centuries ago, have little in common with the original ones. In the fourth century A.D., this low, rocky knoll began to disappear beneath the vault of the Church of the Holy Sepulchre, which was being built over the cave believed to have been Christ's brief, final resting place. The original building has undergone all sorts of indignities as a result of changes in political rule, including demolition, fire, and assassinations, but today it enjoys a period of relative peace and quiet—leaving aside the occasionally violent squabbles among the six Christian communities jointly responsible for its administration. At least this place has been of interest only to the believers of a single religion.

The same cannot be said of Mount Moriah, which has been far too popular to have any hope of experiencing peace. Venerated as the site of Abraham and Isaac's adventures, Mount Moriah is revered all the more fervently by the Jews thanks to the temple from which it takes

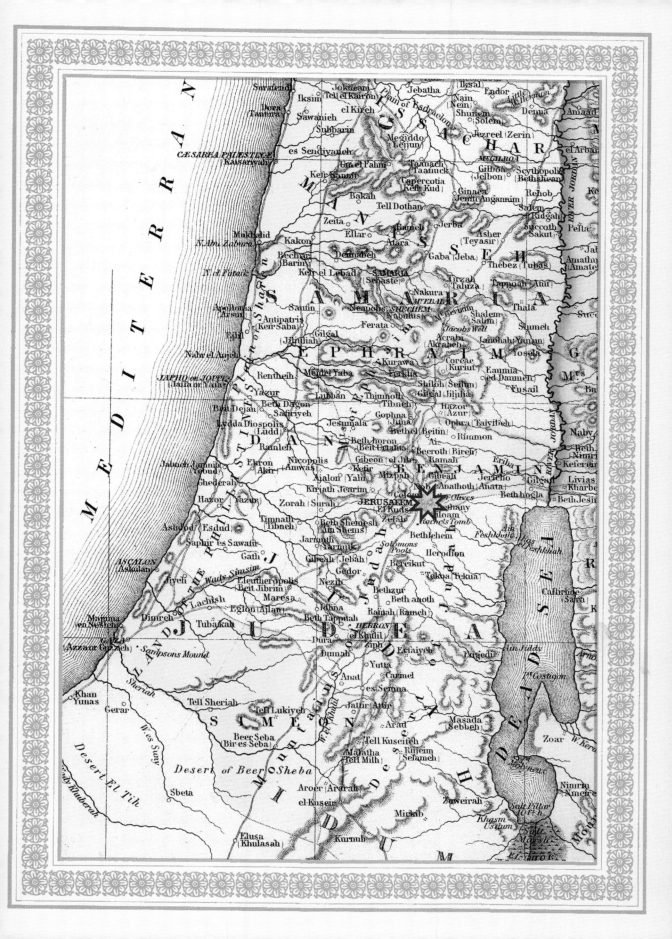

its present-day name. An initial structure known as the Temple of Solomon is thought to have been constructed as early as the tenth century B.C., but has left no trace, other than in the Bible. The second took shape some five centuries later and underwent various changes before reaching its ultimate incarnation as the so-called Temple of Herod, which was in turn destroyed in A.D. 70 by the avenging zeal of Titus's legionnaires. Although nothing has survived of the place of worship as such, what does still exist is the imposing supporting wall erected by Herod in order to buttress the esplanade on which the temple was built. The western part of this wall is appropriately named the Western Wall—but is better known as the Wailing Wall.

In view of the above, it is not difficult to imagine the importance of Temple Mount to the Jews: It is, quite simply, the holy of holies. As luck would have it, the Christians did not enter into competition with them over this site. Although having a clear interest in it (think of Isaac and Christ's visits to the temple), even to the point of possibly having erected a church there during the Byzantine era (archaeologists are divided over this), they laid no special claim to this spot. Islamic interest in the site was no more inevitable, as the Muslims situated the sacrifice of Isaac in Saudi Arabia along with their other main holy sites: Mecca, Muhammad's place of birth in around 570, and Medina, where his tomb is located. Alas, although there

is no mention of Jerusalem in the Qur'an, tradition nevertheless has it that Temple Mount was one of the main stages in the Isra and Mi'raj, the Prophet's fantastic nocturnal journey during which he is said to have flown to heaven accompanied by the archangel Gabriel. This was to bring Temple Mount a new status as Islam's third most holy site and the new names Haram al-Sharif (or the Noble Sanctuary) and the Esplanade of Mosques, due to the presence there of the Dome of the Rock and the Al-Aqsa Mosque, constructed one after the other at the end of the seventh century. And at the same time, it brought restricted access for non-Muslims in the spirit of "to each his or her own place," which could also perhaps be interpreted in this case as "each in turn."

Recurrent dreams of hegemony have brought continual destruction and bloodshed to the region ever since the Middle Ages. The political exploitation of every page of the sacred texts and of every stone unearthed only reinforce further the hopelessness of the impasse. Nefarious spirits from all over the world prowl around these tired walls, condemning Jerusalem to the role of eternal obstacle to peace. It is as if the Middle East were lacking in other magnificent hills and other sites conducive to lifting one's soul heavenward, to praising the beauty of creation and honoring its author. It seems that mankind is capable of transforming even the most beautiful holy stories into a nightmare.

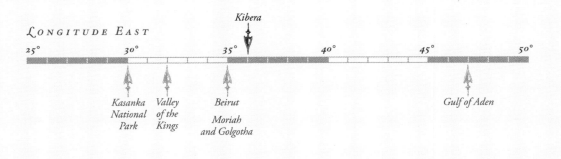

LONGITUDE EAST

25°   30°   35°   Kibera   40°   45°   50°

Kasanka   Valley   Beirut   Gulf of Aden
National   of the
Park   Kings   Moriah
                       and Golgotha

1°18′S – 36°47′E

KIBERA

AN UNCHARTED CESSPOOL

inding a detailed map of this Kenyan agglomeration that is home to a million wretched souls is nearly impossible. Cartographers know so little about the place that they prefer to simply ignore its existence. Besides, how can a surging mass devoid of any administrative reality—and dangerous, to boot—be surveyed? And what possible need could there be for a map of this shantytown, even if it is the largest in Africa? No state official, no domestic appliance salesperson, and certainly no tourist could have the remotest reason for venturing, at considerable personal risk, into this maze of muddy alleyways and metal sheeting.

Although lacking any satisfactory representation, this place has a somewhat deceptive name: The Nubi word *kibera* means "forest," not that one would be able to find any plant structures of that type here. This name relates to a period exactly a century ago, when Nubian soldiers from the British Empire's colonial battalions were allocated plots of land on the outskirts of Nairobi in what, at that time, indeed still resembled a forest. The situation remained relatively stable until the beginning of the 1960s, with around five thousand people

> *In no other place on earth are so many humans crammed into such a small space.*

living here, a perfectly reasonable population density given the settlement's area of less than a square mile. Twenty years later, the population had increased tenfold as a result of a massive exodus from the countryside. By the beginning of the 1990s, this population had quadrupled, and it would continue to double every ten years, hence the disappearance of the trees in order to make room for people. In no other place on earth are so many humans crammed into such a small space: an estimated five hundred thousand per square mile, with an average of ten people inhabiting every room. With no reliable supply of drinking water, largely inadequate sanitary facilities, and exponential criminality, shantytowns are a form of no-man's-land bursting with human life, and Kibera is no exception. However, the absence of any legal status does not mean that nothing goes on here. Beneath the sheet-metal roofs an extremely dynamic informal economy has developed, with bakers, joiners, tailors, and the hiring out of all sorts of items, even cell phones. To this list can be added a number of less commendable activities, from racketeering to the trafficking of a bewildering variety of goods and the settling of

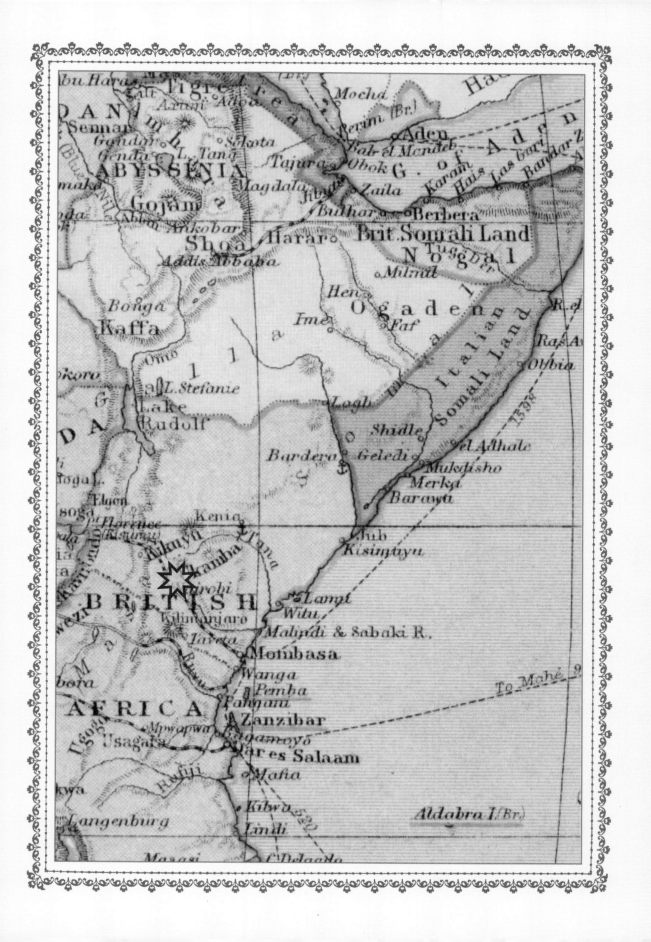

political or organized crime scores to ethnic clashes.

And as in every other suburb in the world, many Kibera residents leave their meager home each morning to earn a living in the capital. The most direct and reliable route to the city center is along the railway track that passes through the shantytown, and as a result thousands of people can be seen trekking along the ballast at daybreak and again at night. Due to tiredness and the dark, the tragically discreet locomotives frequently perform the Grim Reaper's work; statistics are no longer kept of accidents in which absentminded walkers are hit by a train.

Nevertheless, the inhabitants need to work because, contrary to what one might imagine, the cost of living in hell is relatively high. No one can lay claim to authentic land ownership in Kibera because occupation of the area has been illegal for the last few decades. However, this doesn't stop certain local "godfathers" from doing excellent business managing sections of the settlement as if they were officially registered plots of land. To rent a simple room can cost twelve dollars per month, a significant amount for people whose monthly salary is seldom more than twenty-seven dollars. Altogether, this business must generate an annual turnover in the region of $9.5 million for the whole of Kibera.

The inhabitants have little choice. Whether they are seasonal migrants or permanent workers earning too little to allow them to obtain proper accommodation, they are condemned to molder in this cesspool and hand over a large proportion of their meager resources to the sharks of Kibera. And because it never rains but it pours, the shantytown is surrounded on all sides by comfortable homes as if to serve as a permanent reminder of what a normal life would be like. Dreamers can even fantasize about a magnificent green space directly bordering the northern boundary of the slum: the Royal Nairobi Golf Club, which has spread its lawns over a space into which Kibera's ingenious engineer-builders could no doubt squeeze at least 150,000 people. The most optimistic could always claim that there is a good side to all this wretchedness: AIDS infection—and the practice of prostitution—has reached such high levels that the extraordinarily bad sanitary conditions have convinced clinics and practitioners to come and set up shop inside the area.

Regarding the myopia of maps, there is a glimmer of hope here too. The lay of the land is gradually emerging thanks to an initiative known as the Map Kibera Project, launched by an Italian researcher with the assistance of residents of the shantytown and various Kenyan universities. Based on the principle that formalization of a problem is the first step toward finding a solution, this nongovernmental organization has undertaken a methodical evaluation of the area comprising a census, the statistical analysis of problems and needs, and appropriate mapping. Might this finally bring these forgotten people to attention and open up a less grim future for them?

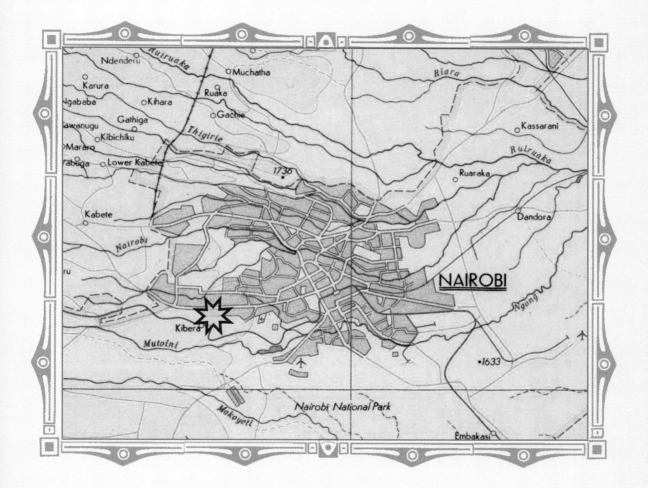

FROM THE BARENTS SEA TO THE INDIAN OCEAN

ZAPADNAYA LITSA

＊

GULF OF ADEN

＊

GUR-EMIR

＊

THILAFUSHI

69°26′N – 32°23′E

ZAPADNAYA LITSA

THE ANTECHAMBER OF HELL

In the extreme northwest of Russia, close to the Norwegian border, there exists a kind of paradise for lovers of raw nature. Or is the vast Kola Peninsula actually the antechamber of hell? Not simply because of its terrible weather conditions and interminable polar night, nor even because visitors regularly need to shut their eyes to avoid the sinister sight of naval installations abandoned after the collapse of the Soviet system: dozens of ghost towns, hideous blocks of concrete with smashed windows, vacant factories, abandoned metal carcasses of all kinds strewn over the ground. No, of all these desolate, snow-covered relics from the past, the most dreadful are not the most visible. The real danger lurks at the bottom of Russia's northern fjords. From the heights surrounding the magnificent Litsa Fjord, thirty-seven miles northwest of Murmansk, one can see the enormous nuclear submarines, weary but incredibly dangerous, with which the country no longer knows what to do, neatly lined up along the banks like harmless museum exhibits. To give a sense of the scale of the problem: Concentrated in this one place is a quantity of radioactive fuel thirty times greater than that of the Chernobyl reactor.

> *The real danger lurks at the bottom of Russia's northern fjords.*

During its glory days, the USSR maintained a fleet of 247 nuclear-powered submarines. Of the 192 that have since been retired, only a little more than half have been broken up in compliance with the proper procedures. The others continue to gently rust away, most of them at the Zapadnaya Litsa naval base, under the worried gaze of scientists monitoring the risk of leaks with whatever tools they have at their disposal and attempting to evaluate the consequences of one or two of the subs sinking or—heaven preserve us—of a catastrophic spontaneous chain reaction.

Hopefully it will not come to that, because the European governments have sized up the time bomb and chosen to assist Russia—financially as well as technically—in neutralizing the danger. A more "sensible" storage site has been established in Sayda Bay at the entrance to Murmansk Fjord, where the reactors are dismantled and made safe, but it will no doubt take another two decades and a great deal of money before the dangerous remnants of Russia's Northern Fleet are disposed of once and for all.

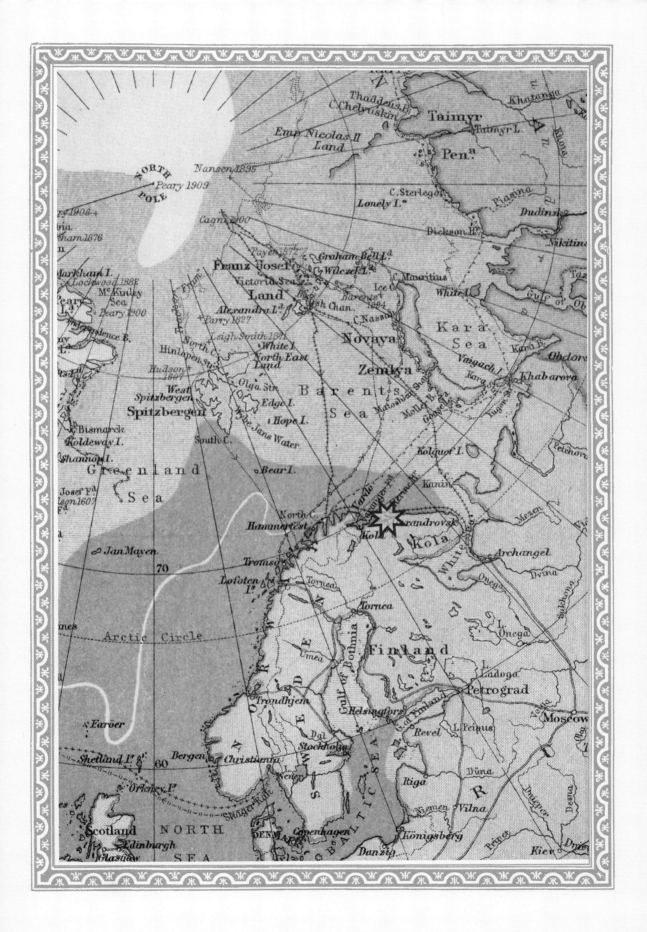

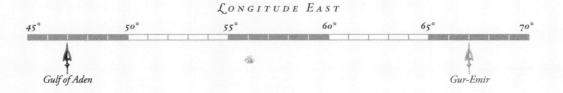
12° N – 47° E

GULF OF ADEN

HUNTING GROUND OF PIRATES

The blinding light in which Cape Guardafui is bathed is not to be trusted. Nor are the glinting turquoise waves that break on the light-colored rock, or the immaculate spume of the waves that the powerful monsoon winds drive into the strait in tight rows. The extreme tip of the Horn of Africa conceals its perils beneath picture-postcard hues. There are no holiday resorts, and visitors are not greeted with garlands of flowers when they arrive; there are no thousand-year-old monuments to photograph or cruise programs offering excursions to picturesque sites.

It's just the opposite—a cruel game whose rules please no one but apply to all, spreading misery both at sea and on land, among locals and travelers alike. It's impossible to know who to pity in this spiral of bad faith: the sailors taking this route gripped by fear and occasionally paying for the privilege with several months of captivity in inhumane conditions, or even with their lives? Or the notoriously poor Somalis to whom the local employment agency has little to offer other than piracy?

Strictly speaking, there's nothing new about piracy. It has prospered on all five continents since the dawn of time, often playing an important role in the economy of coastal regions, like a less-well-policed version of the toll system officially operated along shorelines and rivers. Contrary to popular opinion, piracy did not disappear with the rise of globalization during the second half of the twentieth century. It simply relocated to the parts of the world best suited to this kind of activity. Pirates, just like conventional entrepreneurs, need the right combination of factors in order to succeed: an ample sufficiency of commercial traffic, a cheap and motivated workforce, the appropriate geography and, of course, the absence of any forces of law and order capable of obstructing free market practices.

Somalia, a country of ten million citizens (a quarter of whom have been driven out of their homes), has been in the grips of chronic instability for more than a century and has continually been put to fire and sword by the nine rival factions battling for power. Plus, the zeal of the numerous foreign trawler factory ships operating around Puntland over the last few decades has reduced fish stocks to such an extent that many Somali fishermen have left the trade. Since agriculture offers little in the way of career prospects in this drought-stricken land, it comes as no surprise that some of these former fishermen have turned their interest to the twenty thousand vessels that pass along the 1,880-mile coast each year, sailing for or from the Suez Canal via the Red Sea.

Calling themselves *badaadinta badah*, or "saviors of the sea," many of these pirates believe

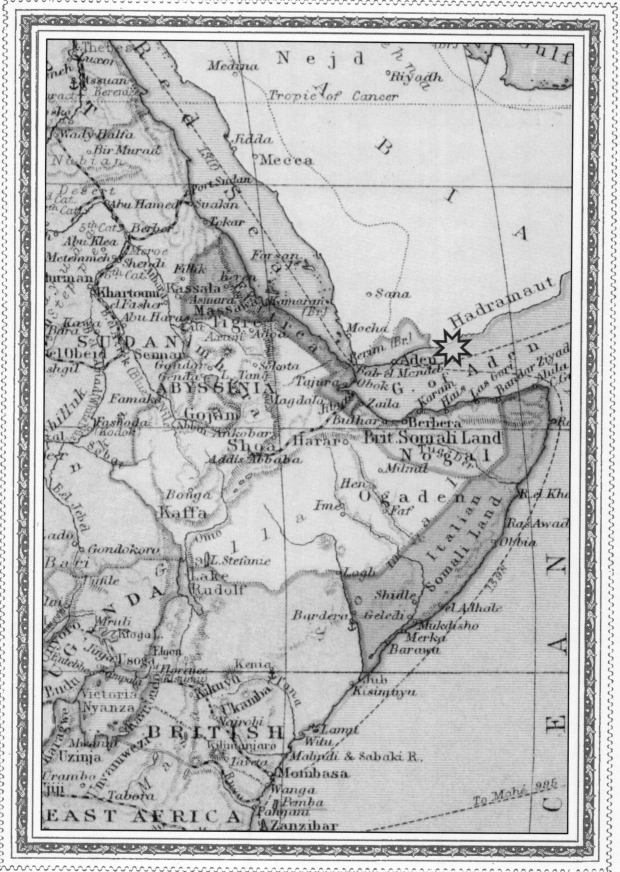

Calling themselves badaadinta badah, *or "saviors of the sea," many of these pirates believe that they are protecting their native waters.*

that they are protecting their native waters and that the hijackings are a form of taxation. In small and swift skips, the attack group approaches the target from all sides, firing their weapons into the air. When they pull close to their target, they throw hooked rope ladders onto the decks and board, taking the ship hostage for ransom.

Logically enough, international organizations are frustrated by these attacks and the amounts demanded in ransom money for the restitution of ships and crews. This has resulted in the implementation of various surveillance measures, including Operation Atalanta. Since its inception in 2008, this initiative, which has the blessing of the UN, has mobilized the navies of thirteen European countries, chiefly those of France, Germany, and Spain.

Initially these measures resulted in a significant dispersion of the problem. In order to evade the vigilance of the participating navies, the pirates moved farther and farther away from the Gulf of Aden itself to attack shipping in unexpected places: near the Seychelles, by the entrance to the Persian Gulf, and even in the middle of the Indian Ocean, up to 1,200 miles from their bases.

But business is not what it was. Tracked by European frigates, the pirates gradually launched fewer and fewer attacks, and those they did carry out were less likely to succeed. At the end of the first decade of the new millennium, they had succeeded in taking up to fifty vessels and more than one thousand sailors hostage. By the beginning of 2013, this figure had fallen to four ships and a hundred or so crew, resulting in a clear downturn in the pirates' earnings: a "mere" $33 million in ransom revenues in 2012 compared to $142 million a year before. However, it would take only a withdrawal by the warships for the pirates to retake possession of these immense hunting grounds.

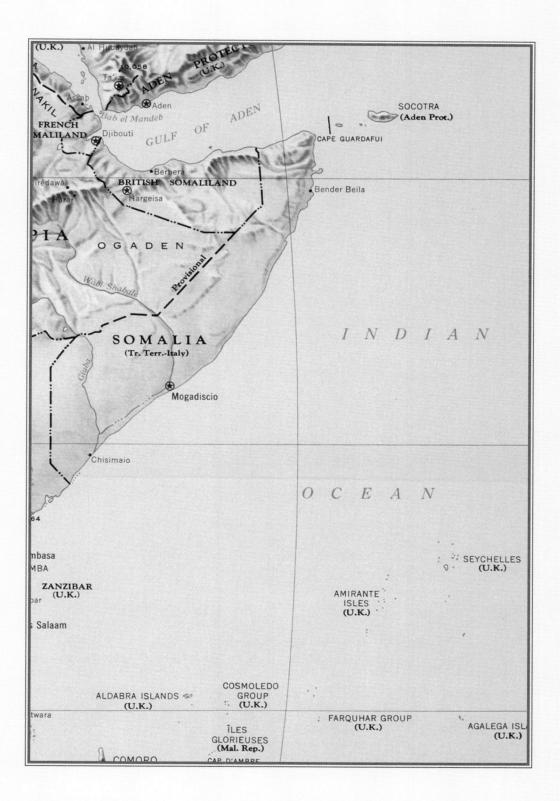

39°40′ N – 67° E

GUR-EMIR

THE MALEVOLENT MAUSOLEUM

To succeed in slaying seventeen million people at a time when the world population was barely more than three hundred million reveals a certain talent for the art of massacre—all the more so when one stops to consider that the rustic nature of transportation in the fourteenth century and the absence of any weapons of mass destruction significantly complicated the task of genocide. Nevertheless, such was the death toll achieved during his reign by Timur, who in Samarqand in 1360 became emir of what was then Transoxiana, a land located between the Amu and Syr rivers—in other words, current-day Uzbekistan along with some of Kazakhstan. This indefatigable killer journeyed, sword in hand, from the foothills of the Himalayas to Turkey, making a thorough exploration of Persia and memorable incursions into India along the way. The chronicles of his conquests serve as a reminder that in those days it was better to be a skilled craftsman than a peasant: Intent upon embellishing his capital, Timur was careful to spare and bring to Samarqand anyone who could serve his ambitions. In keeping with a custom greatly in vogue at the time, the rest of the civilian population was casually put to the sword.

When I rise from the dead, the world shall tremble.

It was thanks to this international cooperation that a number of magnificent edifices were built, including the Gur-Emir mausoleum, commissioned by Timur as the resting place of his favorite grandson, who was killed in combat in 1403.

Designed to be the most sumptuous of tombs, with its slabs of onyx, exquisite decoration, and a dome rising to a height of some 105 feet, the mausoleum would also subsequently accommodate the grandfather. A mysterious legend grew up around an inscription on its walls, which has been interpreted as meaning: "When I rise from the dead, the world shall tremble." This is by no means the first-ever enigmatic phrase linked to a great sovereign. The problem here was that the Russian forensic scientist Mikhail Gerasimov developed a fascination for Timur and, seeking to prove that he was a descendant of Genghis Khan, undertook to exhume and study the conqueror's remains.

On June 22, 1941, a few hours after the opening of the tomb, Germany launched an attack on the Soviet Union. If a link were established between the famous Operation Barbarossa and the exhuming of Timur, another thirty million victims would need to be added to the seventeen million already mentioned.

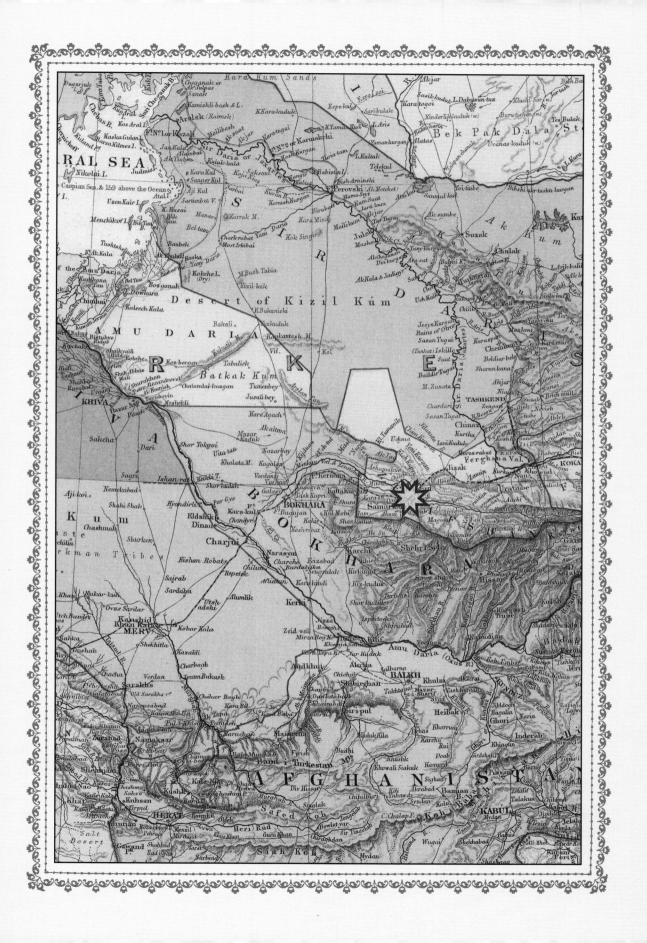

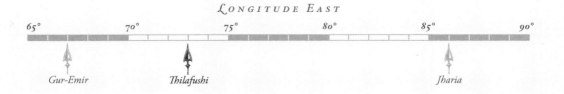
4°11´E – 73°26´E

THILAFUSHI

THE TOXIC LAGOON

In paradise, as in the real world, someone is always needed to put the trash out. And when the garbage disposal services are overloaded, you realize with horror that you're living in hell. Such is life in the Maldives archipelago, considered by connoisseurs of coconut palms and crystalline water to be one of the most convincing reflections on earth of the Garden of Eden. And they certainly have a point. The Divine Sower who scattered these twenty-six atolls—each comprising dozens of islands—over the Indian Ocean had a wonderful sense of form and color. Hoteliers began to fall in love with the region in the 1970s. These delicate strips of sand bordering shallow lagoons and sheltered from the ocean waves are the perfect venue for lazing around by the sea and are also ideal for the installation of bungalows on stilts, which are adored by the tourists. A hundred island hotels based on a typically local concept of transforming a proportion of the 1,800 uninhabited islets into upmarket tourist complexes have made the nation's name.

The island geography also facilitates segregation by categories of use: the tourists stay on the hotel islands and are not supposed to visit the

"Rafts" of garbage occasionally detach themselves from the island and drift across the magnificient turquoise water.

islands that are home to the Maldivians, who in turn are not allowed to access the hotel islands unless they work there. To each his or her own. And for more than a quarter of Maldivians, "their own" is now the capital Malé, where these new city-dwellers bitterly regret that the Creator, in all his ingenuity, did not better anticipate the problems of space and waste disposal.

Given that the population has doubled to four hundred thousand over the last three decades, that the archipelago welcomes almost eight hundred thousand tourists each year, and that the small island capital alone accommodates more than one hundred thousand souls in an area covering less than three quarters of a square mile, the problem is starting to become a nightmare. In 1992 the authorities believed they had found the perfect solution when they hit upon the ingenious idea of transforming the neighboring island of Thilafushi into a garbage dump. Unfortunately this idea soon was soon severely tested by simple arithmetic. The average inhabitant of Malé produces about six pounds of waste each day, compared to one and a half pounds for those living on the other islands and nine to fifteen pounds per tourist. This means that the

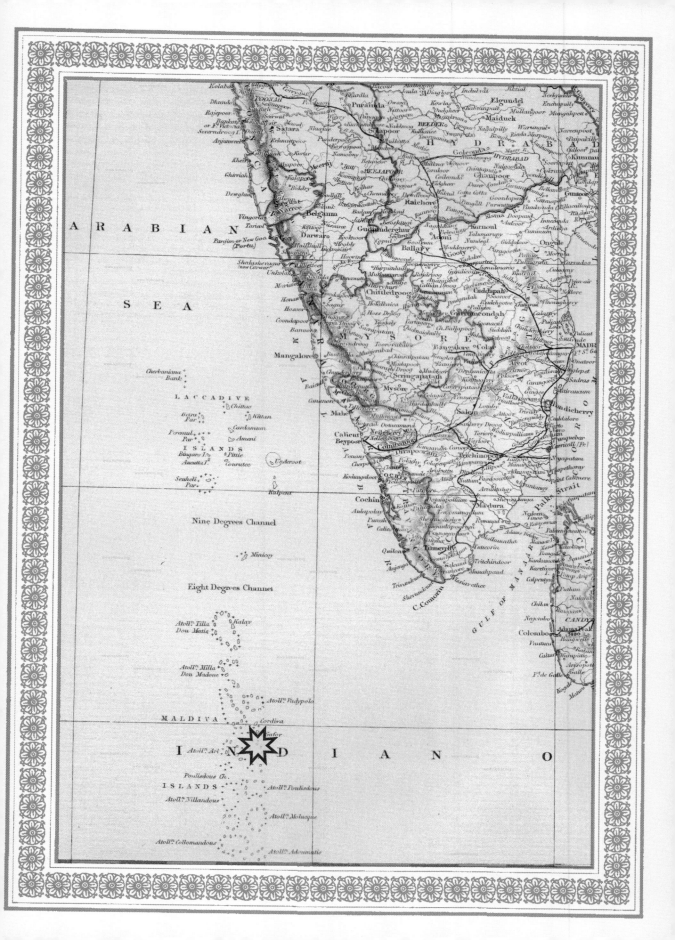

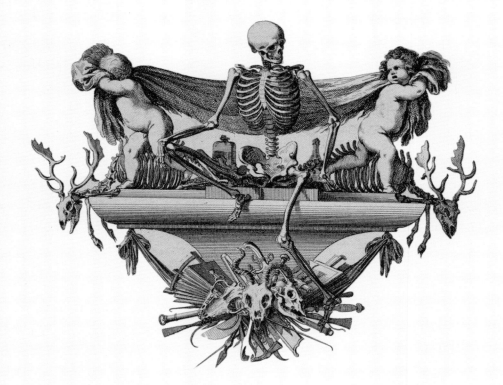

capital needs to convey more than 330 tons of assorted waste every day to Thilafushi, which, despite the best of intentions, is incapable of digesting such large volumes as it is only a narrow loop of land barely more than 650 feet wide. As a result, the island has been overflowing with garbage for the last few years in spite of the best efforts of a gang of Bangladeshi immigrants to burn as much of it as possible, no doubt at the same time relishing the potentially toxic smoke that is given off. To be fair, the capital, less than four miles from Thilafushi, also shares this particular pleasure when the wind is blowing from the west. And the lagoon benefits from the garbage disposal scheme as well: When there's nowhere to stow the latest consignment, why not simply dump it in the shallows that surround the island? This enables Thilafushi to grow day by day, the mountains of garbage usefully extending beyond the sand and coral of the atoll. And it also allows certain noxious substances—heavy metals, batteries, chemical products—to discreetly but surely seep into the

waters of the lagoon. This gives rise to the dispiriting sight of "rafts" of garbage occasionally detaching themselves from the island and drifting across the magnificent turquoise water.

While the Thilafushi open-air garbage dump may be the highly visible abscess of the infection, the issue affects the whole of the archipelago. By distributing the garbage more or less all over the atolls, the tsunami of 2004 boosted awareness of the problem and led to the setting up of twenty-four collection centers. Today almost all are inoperative due to a shortage of personnel and the absence of laws clearly explaining to citizens and businesses what they may and may not do.

However, the nation has more important things to worry about. With a height above sea level of three yards at best, it could be that the sorting of household waste will prove to have been a distraction of distinctly secondary importance once the ocean has risen high enough to engulf the mountains of garbage piled up on Thilafushi.

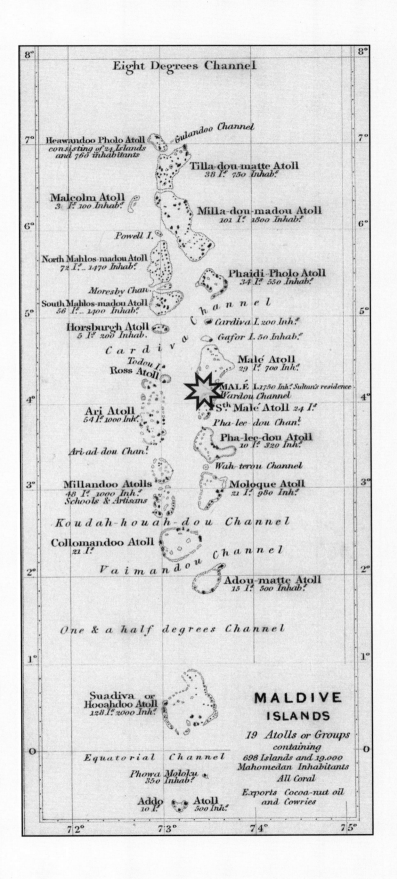

Eight Degrees Channel

Heawandoo Pholo Atoll
*consisting of 24 Islands
and 760 inhabitants*

Gulandoo Channel

Tilla-dou-matte Atoll
38 Is. 750 Inhab.

Malcolm Atoll
3 Is. 100 Inhab.

Milla-dou-madou Atoll
101 Is. 1800 Inhab.

Powell I.

North Mahlos-madou Atoll
72 Is. 1470 Inhab.

Phaidi-Pholo Atoll
34 Is. 550 Inhab.

Moresby Chan.

South Mahlos-madou Atoll
56 Is. 1400 Inhab.

Channel

Horsburgh Atoll
5 Is. 200 Inhab.

Cardiva I. 200 Inh.

Gafor I. 50 Inhab.

Cardiva

Todou I.
Ross Atoll

Malé Atoll
29 Is. 700 Inh.

MALÉ I. *1750 Inh. Sultan's residence*
Wardou Channel

St h Malé Atoll *24 Is.*

Ari Atoll
54 Is. 1000 Inh.

Pha-lee-dou Chan.

Pha-lee-dou Atoll
10 Is. 320 Inh.

Ari-ad-dou Chan.

Wah-terou Channel

Millandoo Atolls
48 Is. 1000 Inh.
Schools & Artisans

Moloque Atoll
21 Is. 980 Inh.

Koudah-houah-dou Channel

Collomandoo Atoll
21 Is.

Channel

Vaimandou

Adou-matte Atoll
15 Is. 500 Inhab.

One & a half degrees Channel

**Suadiva or
Hooahdoo Atoll**
128 Is. 2000 Inh.

MALDIVE
ISLANDS

*19 Atolls or Groups
containing
698 Islands and 19.000
Mahomedan Inhabitants
All Coral*

*Exports Cocoa-nut oil
and Cowries*

Equatorial Channel

*Phowa Mololu
350 Inhab.*

Addo *Atoll*
10 I. *500 Inh.*

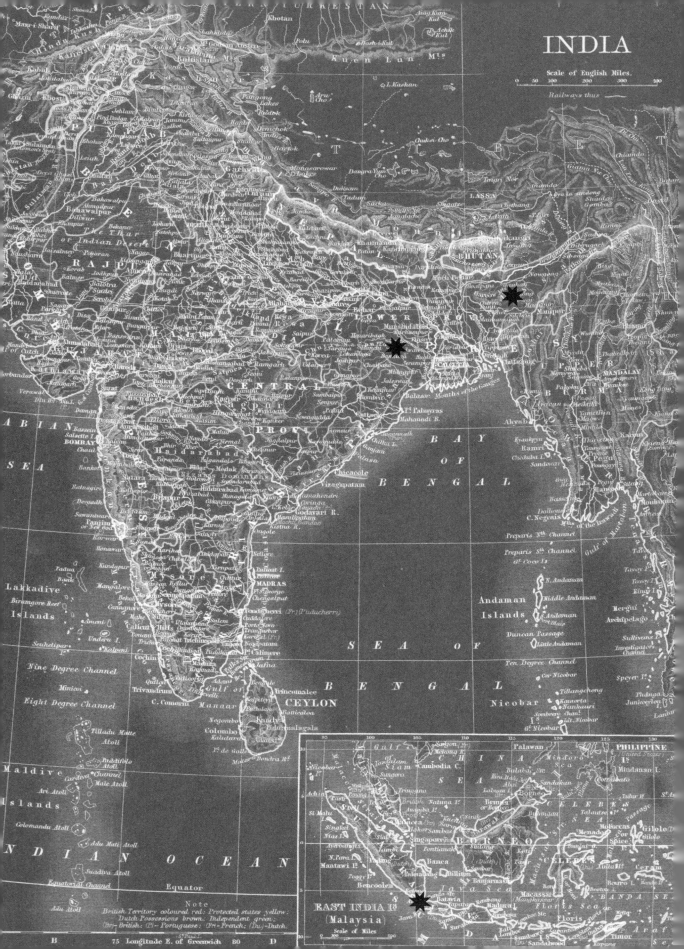

AROUND
THE
BAY OF
BENGAL

JHARIA

✳

JATINGA

✳

SUNDA STRAIT

23°45′N – 86°24′E

JHARIA
UNDERGROUND INFERNO

ere it not for the calm demeanor of the passersby, this place, with its columns of smoke and ravaged landscapes, could be mistaken for a battlefield freshly laid to waste. However, in this district of the state of Jharkhand in northeastern India, the fire does not come from the sky; it has been smoldering below ground for at least a century. There is nothing unusual about this, say the experts: Hundreds of disused coal mines throughout the world experience the same phenomenon. When the hygrometry and temperature are just right, the dust in a poorly sealed pit can burst into flame in even the slightest flow of oxygen. The problem at the Jharia coalfield is that no one knows how to control this steadily expanding underground inferno. Five hundred thousand people live either above or in the immediate vicinity of this enormous furnace that comprises seventy separate blazes and extends over hundreds of acres. At the outset, the inhabitants of the villages around Jharia found a number of advantages in the situation. The mines that weren't burning provided a living for a substantial proportion of the population. The coalfield fires also enabled the villagers to

Buildings collapse as the ground gives way, children disappear down cracks that open up without warning.

economize in certain areas. They only had to place a pot on the outlet of a fissure for the scalding steam from below ground to cook its contents. At a time when Westerners are dreaming of geothermal energy, this may raise a smile. But the local people no longer have the heart to joke.

The ground has reached a temperature of 120°F, toxic fumes seep through the slightest crack, and their homes have become uninhabitable. And that's not all: Buildings collapse as the ground gives way, children disappear down cracks that open up without warning, and the land has become uncultivable.

Sixty-six million tons of coal have already gone up in smoke with no tangible gain other than to make the air of Jharia the most polluted on the subcontinent. The decision to transform some of the underground coal seams into opencast mines has allowed some of the fuel to be recovered, but at the same time it is helping the fires to spread by introducing large quantities of oxygen into the ground. Every local inhabitant knows that their days in the area are numbered: Once the fires have arrived beneath their homes, it will be time to leave.

KATMANDU
Patan
Bhatgaon
Gurkha
Pokhra
Mount Everest
Darjiling
Kampa-dzong
Chitawana
Makwanpur
Bettia
Motihari
Darbhanga
Muzaffarpur
Lalganj
Chapra
Hajipur
Dinapur
Bankipur
Monghyr
Bhagalpur
Purnea
Dinajpur
Rajmahal
English Bazar
Behar
Gaya
Sherghati
Hazaribagh
Siranpur
Naya Dumka
Murshidabad
Barhampur
Suri
Asansol
Raniganj
Purulia
Bankura
Burdwan
Ranchi
Bishnupur
Hooghly
Chinsura
Chandarnagar
Serampur
Howrah
Midnapore
Tamluk
Chaibasa
Bamanghata
Mayurbhanj
Balasore
Keunjhar
Bonaigarh
Sambalpur
Jashpurnagar
Daltonganj
Hazaribagh
Santal Parganas
Birbhum
Purnea
Tarai
Diamond Harbour
Nadia
Plassey
Kalna
Santipur

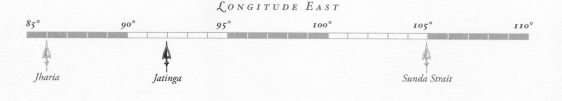
25°6′N – 92°56′E

JATINGA
A PLAGUE OF BIRDS

Why on earth do thousands of birds come and die in this precise spot in the Barail Mountain Range in northeastern India every year? The region boasts landscapes with verdant hills, vast forests, and rivers meandering through majestic valleys; there's certainly no shortage of welcoming sites hereabouts. But it is at Jatinga, an isolated village in the state of Assam, that the birds perish, a state of affairs that has been puzzling ornithologists for the last few decades. The same scenario is enacted every year at the end of the summer after the monsoon: On moonless nights, clouds of birds hurtle into the village lights, and if they don't succeed in killing themselves, the local inhabitants finish them off with bamboo sticks.

Observers have been quick to cast the Jatinga villagers in the role of villain and have accused them of deliberately trapping the unfortunate creatures, lying in wait with their poles after having switched on every available light in order to attract them. There's no doubt that the residents take advantage of the opportunity, doing everything they can to ensure that as much of this godsend as possible ends up in the pot, but they clearly have little to do with the enduring attraction that Jatinga has for these birds.

Scientists have conducted all sorts of experiments, including setting up lights in different locations, but all in vain: The phenomenon can be observed only on the Jatinga ridge. And only under specific conditions. The experts have noticed that it occurs almost exclusively in the early evening, when there's a southerly wind blowing and visibility is poor due to mist or thick clouds. And the birds in question are always approaching from the north—in other words, flying into the wind. Around forty different, mainly local, species are affected: emerald doves, kingfishers, egrets, bitterns, herons, Indian pittas, partridges. Many end up on the ground in Jatinga, with any survivors generally in such a dazed state that they refuse to take any food and die of starvation. Even various species known for their sensible habit of flying in orderly formations seem to be completely disoriented when they arrive in the skies above Jatinga.

In the absence of any better explanation, some people have referred to the severe turbulence that often makes it difficult to fly in the mountains. But why Jatinga in particular? After all, it is only seven hundred meters above sea level, whereas the region is dotted with peaks more than fifteen hundred meters high and far more difficult to negotiate. Might the reason, as some have suggested, be a local magnetic anomaly? Waves capable of interfering with even the most efficient instinctive navigation systems? What remains beyond doubt is that while the researchers continue to construct their hypotheses, the birds will continue to rain down on Jatinga.

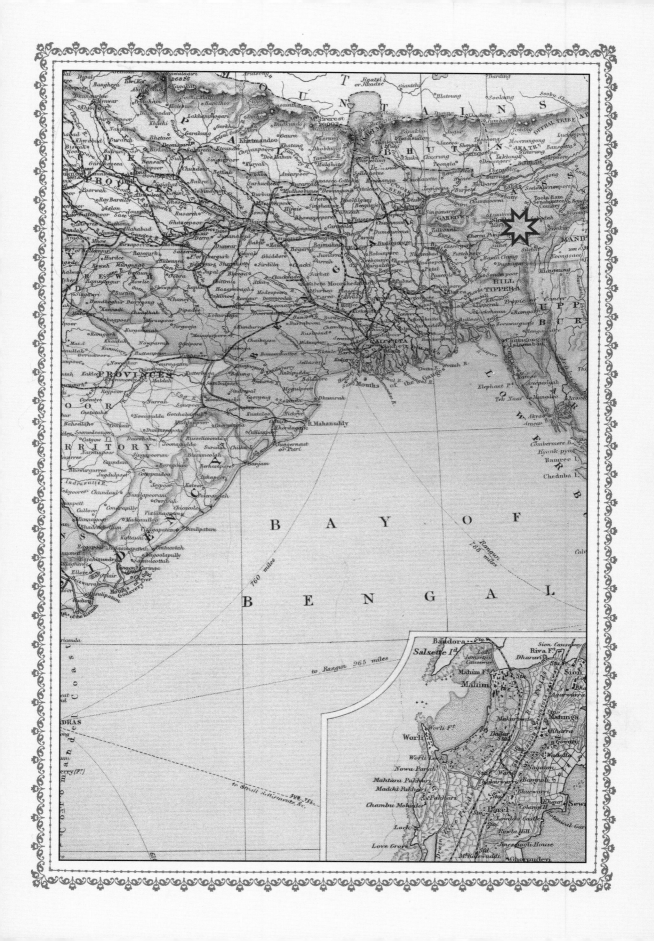

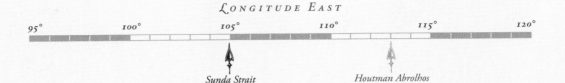
6°08′S – 105°17′E

SUNDA STRAIT

THE MONSTER OF KRAKATOA

The sinister strait separating the islands of Java and Sumatra strikes fear into all who approach it, travelers as well as Indonesians born on its shores. Foreign sailors are never particularly keen to risk their lives in this channel dotted with shallows and oil installations, to say nothing of illegal immigrant trafficking and piracy (about twenty attacks are recorded here every year).

The locals do not spend a lot of time worrying about pirates. By contrast they care very much about the mood swings of the volcano Krakatoa, which has caused a catastrophe or two in the past and continues to display an impressive level of activity. The first officially recorded eruption goes back to A.D. 416 (or A.D. 535 according to some interpretations of the local chronicles). This cataclysm split the original volcano into three separate islands and devastated the entire region, with most of the coastal dwellers drowning in a tsunami generated by the explosion.

In 1883 there was another upheaval. After three months of eruptions and tremors, during which ships passing through the strait were forced to navigate by guesswork in a thick cloud of ash, the volcano exploded between August 26 and 27, producing a detonation that could be heard three thousand miles away and a shockwave that could be felt in Europe. Ash and pumice were spewed over more than three hundred thousand square miles, an area bigger than France. Waves one hundred feet high crashed onto the coast and the tsunami wave lapped the planet three times. The official death toll was put at forty thousand in a region that was then relatively sparsely populated.

Captain W. J Watson of the British ship *Charles Bal* was within the Sundra Straits when Krakatoa became an active volcano:

"The blinding fall of sand and stones, the intense blackness above and around us, broken only by the incessant glare of varied kinds of lightning and the continued explosive roars of Krakatoa, made our situation a truly awful one. At 11 P.M., having stood off from the Java shore, wind strong from the south-west, the island, west-north-west, eleven miles distant, became more visible, chains of fire appearing

> *Waves one hundred feet high crashed onto the coast and the tsunami wave lapped the planet three times.*

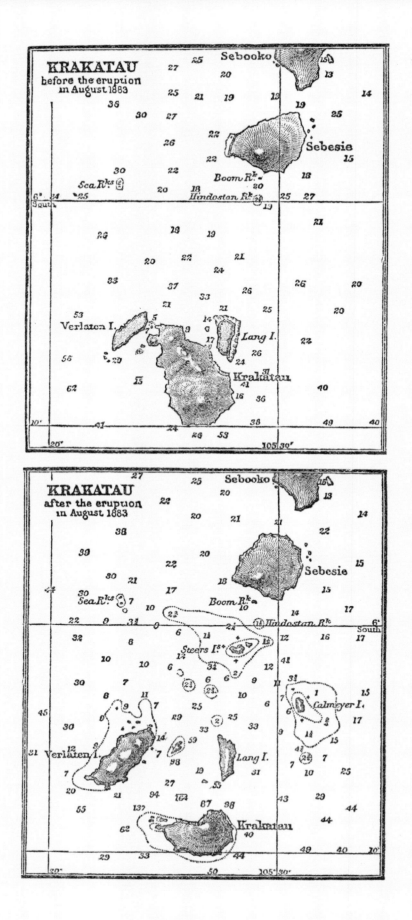

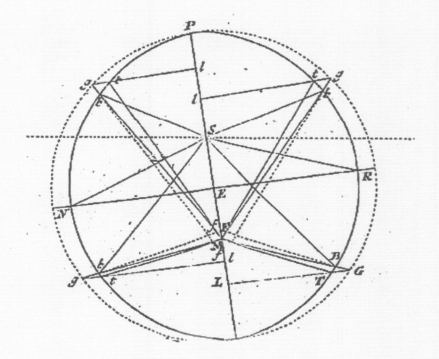

to ascend and descend between the sky and it, while on the south-west end there seemed to be a continued roll of balls of white fire; the wind, though strong, was hot and choking, sulfurous, with a smell as of burning cinders."

Today, six million people live within a radius of sixty-two miles around Krakatoa, and the many "minor" eruptions that continue to enliven the strait prove that the volcano has lost nothing of its vigor. It even gave birth in 1927 to a new island: Anak Krakatoa—the "child of Krakatoa"—

has emerged gradually from the ocean over the years, attaining a height of more than forty feet the day after it first appeared and exceeding one thousand feet today.

Against this peaceful backdrop, with a renewal of seismic activity noted in the 2010s, an $11 billion contract has just been signed for the construction of an enormous suspension bridge (nineteen miles long) connecting Java and Sumatra—just thirty miles from Krakatoa and very close to the underwater fault against which the Indo-Australian plate is pressing with a persistence that borders on obstinacy.

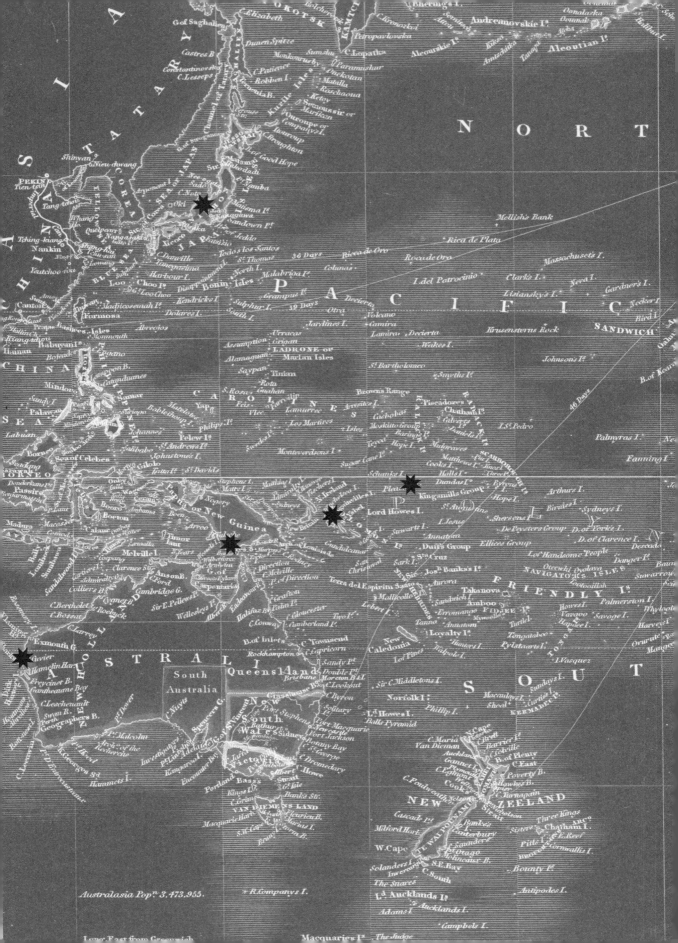

BETWEEN THE ORIENT AND OCEANIA

HOUTMAN ABROLHOS

✳

AOKIGAHARA

✳

CAPE YORK

✳

TAKUU

✳

NAURU

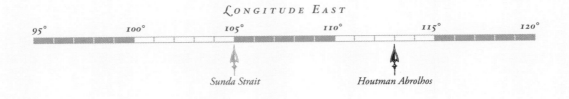
28°43′S – 113°47′E

HOUTMAN ABROLHOS
MASSACRE OF THE SHIPWRECKED

The low-lying islands of the Indian Ocean have a special talent for attracting the evil eye. The story of the 160 slaves abandoned on Tromelin Island after being shipwrecked in 1761 is well known: Just eight of them were still alive when it eventually occurred to someone to send help fifteen years later. The Houtman Abrolhos archipelago, a notorious snare at the eastern extremity of the same ocean, offers an even bleaker picture in terms of horror and macabre number crunching.

No one had heard of these 122 small islands surrounded by reefs, located forty miles off the coast of Australia, before the *Batavia*—a ship of the Dutch East India Company bound for Java—was smashed to pieces there on June 4, 1629, with 320 on board. A number of sailors drowned while trying to reach the shore, but the worst was yet to come. Captain Ariaen Jacobsz and the company representative set off in a rowboat with about forty crew to get help, leaving behind the rest of the crew and a number of passengers.

The assistant quartermaster of the *Batavia*, one Jeronimus Cornelisz, took matters in hand to the great misfortune of all concerned. Not only was this former pharmacist a rogue who had been scheming to seize control of the cargo ever since the ship had left port, he was also a deranged murderer. Persuading some of the sailors and soldiers that it would be impossible to feed everyone, he organized the systematic elimination of a proportion of the survivors. Discreetly at first, he set up small colonies on various small islands that he knew to be lacking in fresh water or by nonchalantly drowning the more feeble, and later, once the future victims saw what he was up to, more openly. From that point on, Cornelisz's henchmen did not hesitate to kill by whatever violent means were at their disposal, sparing the women only in order to use and abuse them. The archipelago became a battlefield in which everyone tried to save his or her own skin.

The massacre only came to an end once the *Saerdam*, alerted by the crew of the rowboat, which had eventually reached Java, arrived on the scene a little more than two months after the shipwreck. The officers of the *Saerdam* held a spot trial at the end of which Cornelisz and six of his acolytes were tried and hanged, drawing a line underneath this staggering carnage that was responsible for the deaths of virtually two hundred men and women.

A century later—may history hide its face in shame—another Dutch ship, the *Zeewijk*, which was supposed to be en route to Jakarta, ran aground on the same reefs. This time there was no slaughter of the innocent, but the incident nevertheless claimed a further twenty-six victims—as a result of starvation, thirst, drowning, disease, and all manner of scourges that are tragically part and parcel of being shipwrecked. And once again there was the madness of a single man, Captain Jan Steyns, who was responsible for running his vessel aground as a result of sailing too close to the coast in order to satisfy his desire to see Australia.

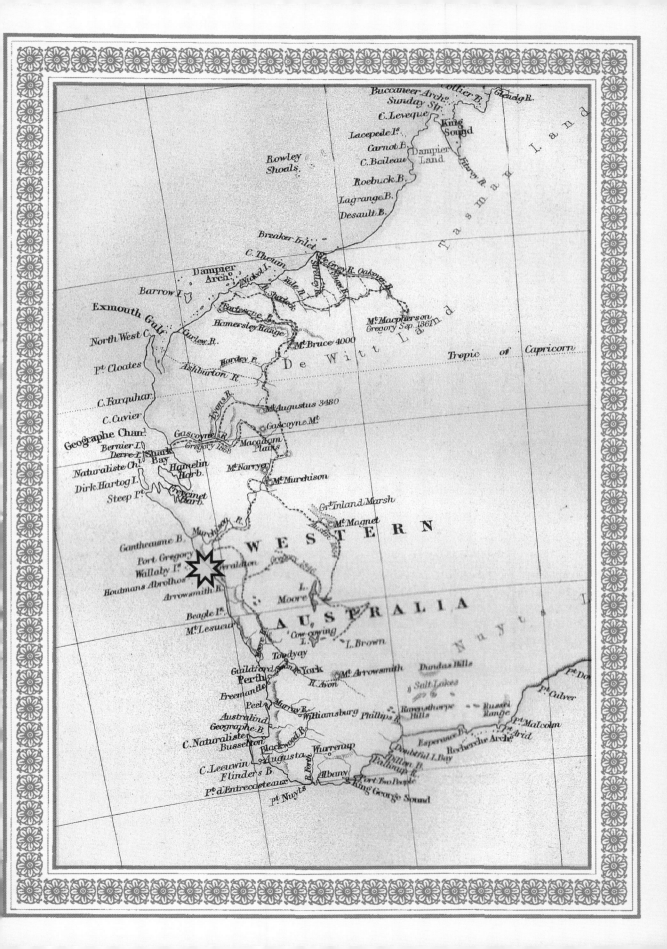

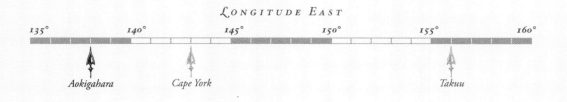
35°28′N – 138°37′E

AOKIGAHARA

THE SUICIDE FOREST

Better to die in a dense forest or in icy waves? The question rarely merits reflection, unless you are considering killing yourself. The answer for many is Aokigahara's disquieting "sea of trees," second in popularity for suicide to San Francisco's famous Golden Gate Bridge. The local Yamanashi Prefecture authorities estimate that around one hundred people come here every year to end their lives in this gloomy forest at the foot of the incredibly photogenic Mount Fuji. However, this may well be an underestimate because, unlike the bridge in California, where fatal jumps rarely lack witnesses, here it is impossible to accurately account for the wretched souls who disappear beneath the canopy of the trees and are never seen again. Only the bodies discovered during the course of systematic annual searches organized by volunteers are entered into the statistics. In addition to the desperate persons themselves, there are also the unlucky and the reckless who enter the forest in order to immerse themselves in the atmosphere of this mysterious place . . . and are unable to find their way out.

Not that the forest is exactly enormous: It covers barely fourteen square miles. But there are few paths, the light is dim due to the density of the vegetation, and the ground is uneven and covered with thick moss concealing deep crevasses, making it difficult to walk. It is also said that compasses go crazy here, that GPS does not work, and that it is impossible to communicate by phone beneath the trees.

Seichō Matsumoto's celebrated novel *Kuroi Jukai* (Black Sea of Trees), published in 1960, is often mentioned in connection with Aokigahara. It is regarded as having made this place famous because two of its characters, two lovers, commit suicide in the forest, thereby signaling that there is no better place in which to end one's life. But the local people know that Death has long prowled these woods and that *yuurei*—the ghosts of the departed who wander the earth in search of paradise—are well acquainted with Aokigahara. And going back more than a century, wasn't *ubasute*, the tradition whereby the elderly would withdraw to an isolated spot to die so as not to be a burden on their families, practiced here? *Ubasute* may no longer be customary, but in spite of the signs at the entrance to the forest seeking to dissuade would-be suicides and the preventative action taken by the Yamanashi volunteers, the morbid lure of Aokigahara remains as strong as ever.

> *The local people know that death has long prowled these woods.*

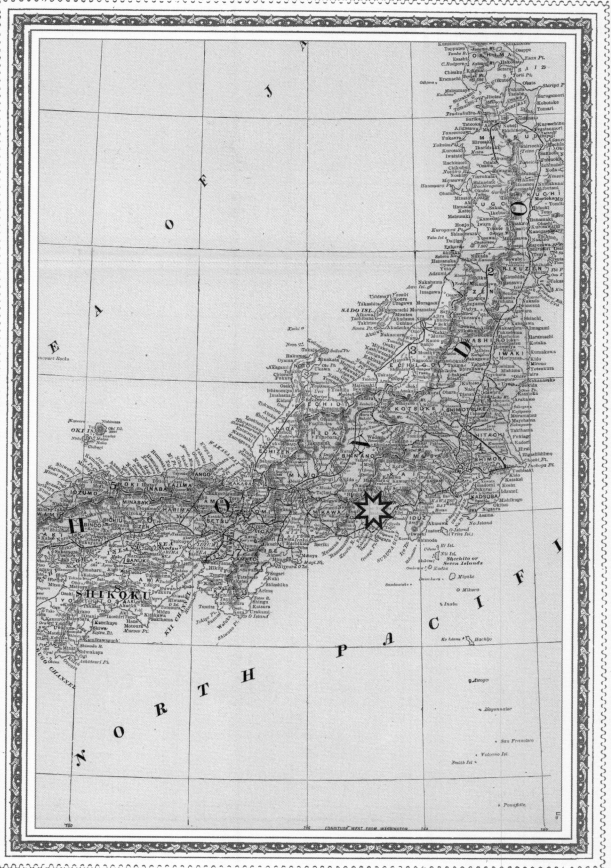

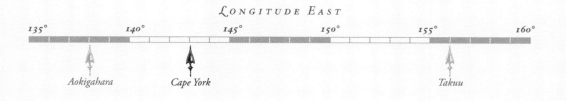
14°48′S – 143°12′E

CAPE YORK

IN THE LAND OF THE KILLER CROCODILES

Cursed? This verdant peninsula situated at the extreme north of Queensland in Australia? Impossible. Among the long beaches of white sand, the turquoise sea populated by corals that occur nowhere else on Earth, and the attractive, practical villas dotted among the lush vegetation you will find no endemic poverty, no insoluble conflict, and no grumbling volcanoes. In fact, the bauxite mines and exploitation of the exceptional fauna and flora that attract countless lovers of the great outdoors every year have brought considerable wealth to the area.

The only problem with this idyllic spot derives from this very same nature, in the form of the largest reptiles in the world. Crocodiles are creatures deserving of respect at the best of times, but these "salties," the local variety, which offer the triple drawback of enjoying the sea while at the same time being both bigger and more aggressive than your normal species. Who wants to swim in a place where there's a danger of encountering voracious monsters sometimes measuring more than seventeen feet? They are known for their explosive attacks from the water and their ability to swim as fast as eighteen miles per hour in short bursts. There is one upside, however, which will no doubt reassure bathers: The local fishermen have noticed that the salties will happily attack, and indeed regularly kill, the dangerous tiger and bull sharks that frequent these waters. Swimming is in any case inadvisable between the end of October and the month of May (unfortunately, this corresponds to the Australian summer, the hottest period of the year) due to the presence of the somewhat irascible box and Irukandji jellyfish. The former is very large (with tentacles up to thirteen feet long) and the latter is minuscule (barely an inch long and therefore difficult to spot), and the stings of either one can be fatal. The jellyfish take time off between June and September, but the sea snakes remain behind—some seventy different species of them, including the delightful *Aipysurus duboisii*, which is regarded as the most venomous of all marine reptiles. While on the subject, it is worth noting that this charming creature is not without competition on dry land: Eight of the ten most dangerous snakes in the world have chosen to take up residence on the peninsula.

It would be unfair, however, to blacken the region's reputation too much: The neighboring areas, bordering the Gulf of Carpentaria, the Sea of Arafura, and the Timor Sea, are in no way inferior to the peninsula where wildlife is concerned. And Cape York remains completely free of the deadly redback spider, which is rife in Australia's more southerly states. *Phew!*

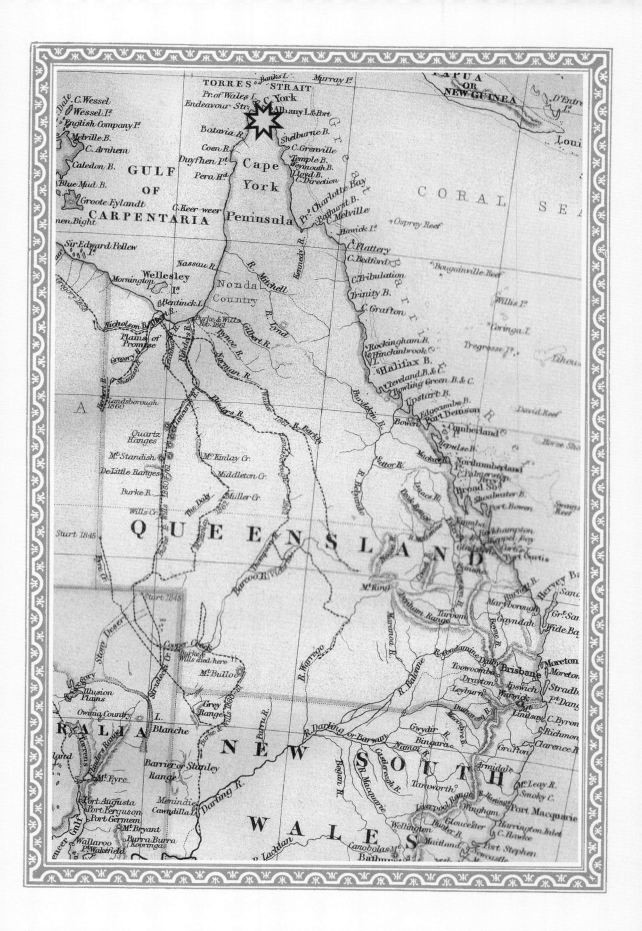

4°45´S – 156°58´E

TAKUU

AN ATOLL LIVING ON BORROWED TIME

The danger facing this isolated atoll can be encapsulated in a typical elementary school exam question: "If Takuu lies a maximum of three feet above sea level and the sea could rise by as much as three millimeters per year, how long will it take for Takuu to become definitively uninhabitable?" Strict arithmetic gives this place, which is home to five hundred souls, another three centuries before it is completely submerged. All that will remain above water are the coconut palms, but it's difficult to imagine a satisfactory community life being organized in the treetops. And should an acceleration occur in the rate at which the sea level is rising, the atoll will have proportionately less time left. What this means is that the inhabitants should not feel they have to wait for a further significant rise in sea level before feeling they need to pack their bags.

To tell the truth, the situation is already beyond critical, and waves have already swept over the island on several occasions. A slightly stronger-than-usual tide or a heavy swell is all it takes for this slender ring of sand and coral to be inundated. Day by day it is becoming more difficult to preserve stocks of fresh water and to grow crops of any kind, as the water table and vegetable gardens have been invaded by salt. And although Takuu is, in principle, safe from cyclones thanks to its proximity to the equator, there is the constant fear that it will find itself in the path of a tsunami like those of 2007 and 2013 that struck the neighboring Solomon Islands.

The islanders of Takuu will therefore need to leave, and they will probably be the first inhabitants of similarly threatened islands to have to resolve to take this step. These people, who have lived in traditional style since time immemorial, six hundred miles from the big cities of their mother country, Papua New Guinea, are disconsolate at the prospect. How can they be expected to acclimatize to the political violence on the island of Bougainville, their nearest potential refuge, or the poverty of Port Moresby, one of the most dangerous cities in the world, having spent so much time living in harmony with the ocean that is now driving them away?

> *There is the constant fear that Takuu will find itself in the path of a tsunami like those of 2007 and 2013 that struck the neighboring Solomon islands.*

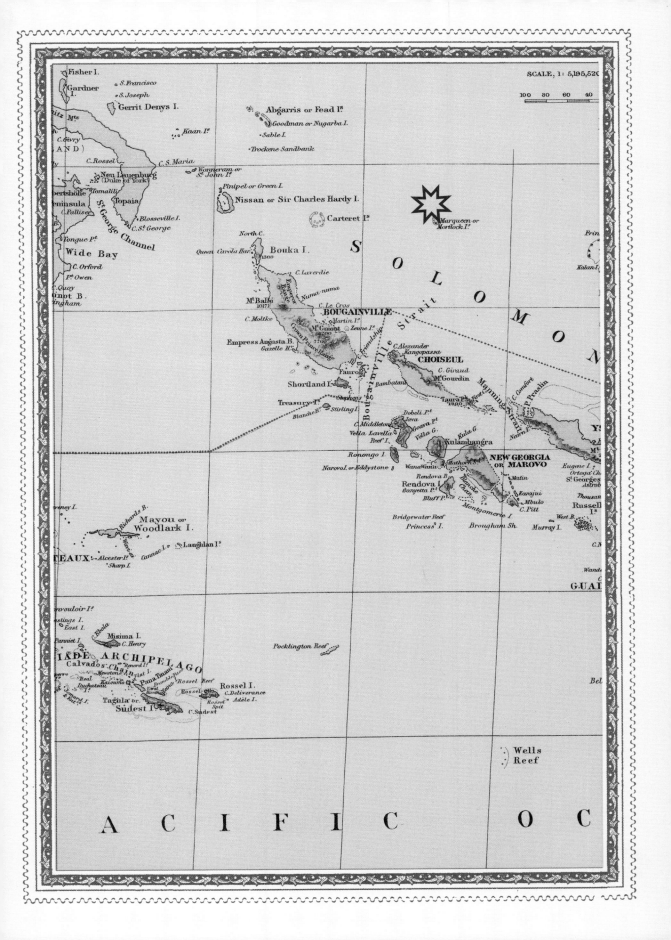

0°31′S – 166°55′E

NAURU

BLIGHTED BY PHOSPHATE

Let us start with one piece of good news: Visitors who are allergic to untamed nature can walk here without fear. On Nauru, mining has been so vigorously pursued for more than a century that almost no trace of flora or fauna remains. All resources, from fuel to water to food, need to be imported. With the exception of the unassuming Nauru reed warbler, an endemic species of modest-sized bird belonging to the *Acrocephalidae* family, the animals one has the most chance of encountering here are cats, dogs, pigs, chickens, and rats, all imported from the neighboring territories.

On the other hand, Nauru has the double distinction of being the smallest republic on the planet (eight square miles with a little more than nine thousand inhabitants) and of having had for a time the second-largest gross domestic product per person after (but not far behind) Saudi Arabia. The emphasis here is very much on the past, because after benefiting from incredible wealth in the 1970s, the Nauruans have since experienced the pain of a descent into hell, their income currently ranking them somewhere below the two hundred mark in terms of GDP, with an unemployment rate over 90 percent and dire problems inherited from when times

were good: 90 percent of the population are overweight, 40 percent are diabetic, and male life expectancy has fallen to fifty-eight years.

The blame is ascribed to the money from mining phosphate, which caused everyone to lose their heads. Having started at the beginning of the twentieth century, under German colonial rule, the mining of this mineral, which derived from a thousand years' worth of fossilized bird droppings, continued after the British Empire took over in 1914 and beyond independence in 1968. But the mines are now nearly stripped.

After having lived the high life, the population discovered in the 1990s that the investments made by their leaders, in anticipation of the end of the mining boom, were worth very little. The facts had to be faced: The cost of maintaining a money pit of an airline that was in any case out of all proportion to the island's needs, disastrous investments, and a generous dose of corruption meant that the coffers were empty. What remained was a landscape devastated by all the mining and a state reduced to having to make ends meet in whatever way it could. Nauru became a tax haven (with several hundred banks domiciled there), then leased part of its modest surface area to Australia as a reception center for illegal immigrants.

> *Good fortune can be a bad counselor.*

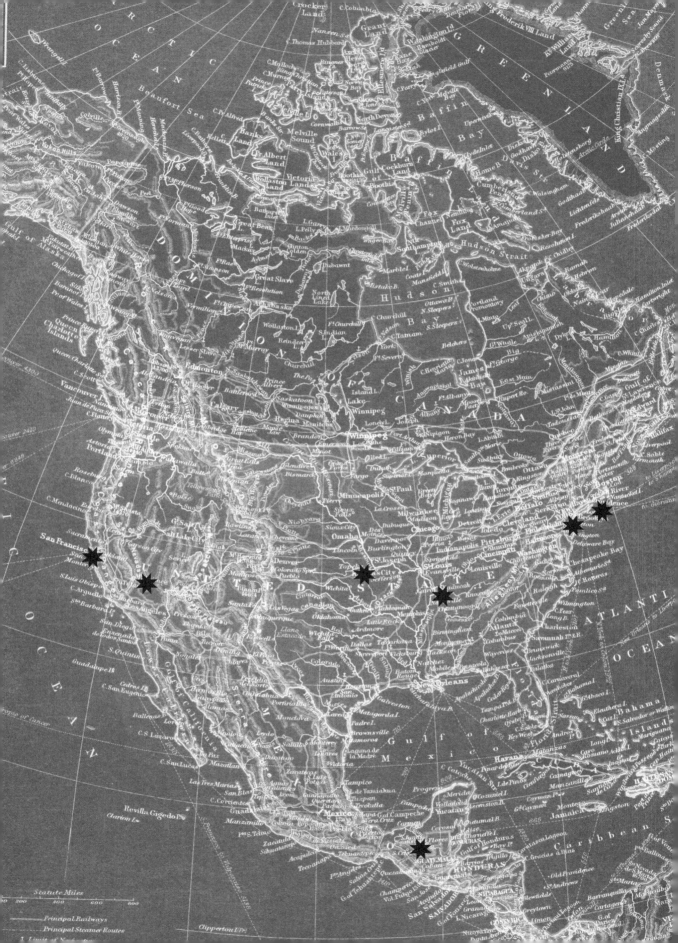

AMERICA FROM COAST TO COAST

MAVERICKS: THE BIG WAVE

✳

NEVADA TRIANGLE

✳

STULL, KANSAS

✳

TONINA

✳

ADAMS, TENNESSEE

✳

PINE BARRENS

✳

AMITYVILLE

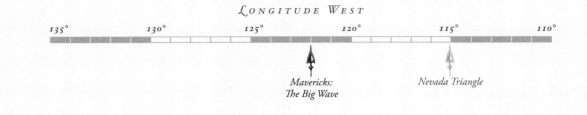
37°29′N – 122°30′W

MAVERICKS: THE BIG WAVE
A COLD-BLOODED MONSTER

There, off Half Moon Bay, some nineteen miles south of San Francisco, a half mile offshore from Pillar Point Harbor, what is perhaps the most dreaded wave anywhere on the planet can be seen breaking. This anomaly of nature feeds both the dreams and the nightmares of every top surfer.

To get an accurate idea of what this place is like, you need to forget all those colorful surf culture clichés, such as palm trees, flower-patterned shirts, white sand, and bikinis. The local beach boys brave the cold water wearing thick black hooded wetsuits. Besides, they don't have time to strut about on the beach because they have to paddle for three-quarters of an hour, avoiding rocks and strong currents, to reach the lineup. It's certainly not the beauty of the scenery that warms their hearts—far from it. This place has nothing in common with the sumptuous turquoise undercroft of Tahiti's Teahupoo or the lightness and delicacy of the waves at Bali or Hawaii. Here, the best they can hope for is a mass of murky water launched at full speed, a dark wall climbing without warning to a height of sixty feet, exploding with such power that it can be recorded on the Richter scale.

This monster would probably have remained unknown had a young and intrepid local boy not tamed it in the 1970s. A high school student from Princeton-by-the-Sea, Jeff Clark, had developed a passion for the great beast that roared nearby when the winter storms generated enough of a swell to rouse it. In 1975, he risked it for the first time, and then a second. Over a period of fifteen years—always alone—he learned the secrets of this atypical wave ignored by the big-wave surfing community, who only had eyes for Hawaii. And then one day Jeff revealed his secret garden to a group of friends, who couldn't believe their eyes. Photos of Mavericks went all around the world, and the elite of the discipline rushed to Princeton-by-the-Sea. Then disaster struck. In December 1994, Mark Foo, the master of big wave riding from Hawaii, drowned here, knocked out by blows from the wave soon after arriving. Mavericks became the cursed wave that would take more lives and cause many more injuries. But it is impossible to avoid: All self-respecting big-wave surfers simply have to pit themselves against it. And so, despite being gripped by fear, they submit to this ultimate surfing challenge that, deep down, nobody wants to take. Giving yourself up to the cold water, getting your bearings as best you can relative to the coast in order to avoid the impact zone, trying not to think about the reefs that just want to break your bones or, even worse, snag the leash of any surfer unlucky enough to be caught in the crusher, thereby condemning him to drown.

For those unmoved by the prospect of being crushed to death between icy water and jagged rocks, there is more danger to be had. Great white sharks of the North Pacific have a particular predilection for the shallows off Pillar Point.

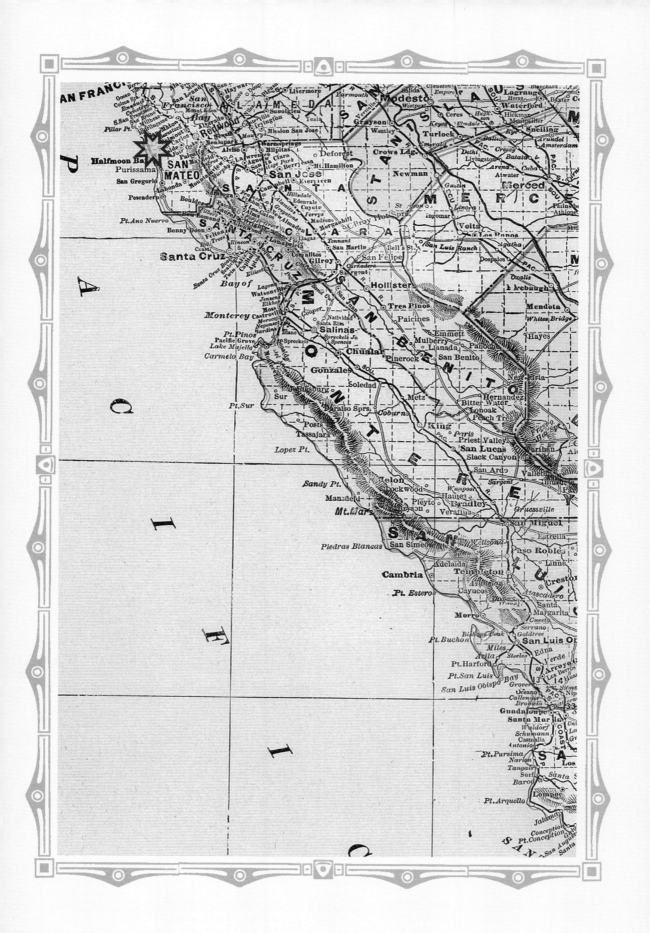

37°14′N – 115°48′W

NEVADA TRIANGLE
A DANGER IN THE SKY

We ought to be far more wary than we are of mirages. They are created mostly by professionals in the tourist industry, a body of people gripped by the mysterious conviction that their clients are incapable of being interested in the reality of the country they long to visit, and that they therefore have to be sold as fantastic a vision of it as possible.

This is no less true of Nevada. Having set off with the intention of exploring a scorching desert graced by outsize casinos, the honest traveler is surprised to observe that the red sand is ringed by snow-capped mountains and impenetrable forests populated by tetchy bears, and to learn that any offer of an excursion by plane should be politely declined as more than two thousand aircraft have gone missing hereabouts over the last five decades, a rate of loss infinitely greater than that of the fabled Bermuda Triangle.

These sinister statistics were of interest to none but the local newspapers until, all of a sudden, one particular news item brought the region to international attention: On September 3, 2007, the billionaire Steve Fossett, well known for his various exploits on the sea and in the sky, went missing during a regular sightseeing flight above the Sierra Nevada. After a month of searching, the authorities decided to call off the search operation without having found either the aviator or his aircraft.

In autumn 2008, a rambler's miraculous discovery of a wallet containing $1,005 and three pieces of identification belonging to Fossett led to the resumption of the investigation. Two days later, air and land searches resulted in the discovery, 730 yards from the same place, of the wreck of the small, single-engine Bellanca N240 R the adventurer had been flying. The DNA analysis of remains recovered nearby removed any remaining doubt that the body was indeed that of Steve Fossett.

The contrast could not have been more striking. A short flight from the reassuring neon of Las Vegas, it was apparently possible for an airplane to vanish into thin air, eluding discovery for a whole year! And the search did not lack effort. In keeping with the fame of the victim, never before had so much money—a figure of more than $2 million, shared between the public authorities and Fossett's friends and family—been spent on searching for an individual on US soil. This enormous mobilization of manpower also produced some unexpected results in the shape of a dozen or so airplane wrecks scattered about the Sierra, to which no one had paid any real attention before then—that is, other than a number of UFO spotters and conspiracy theorists who pointed their finger at a mysterious military installation at the very center of the search zone.

In principle, there's nothing particularly surprising about siting a US Air Force base in

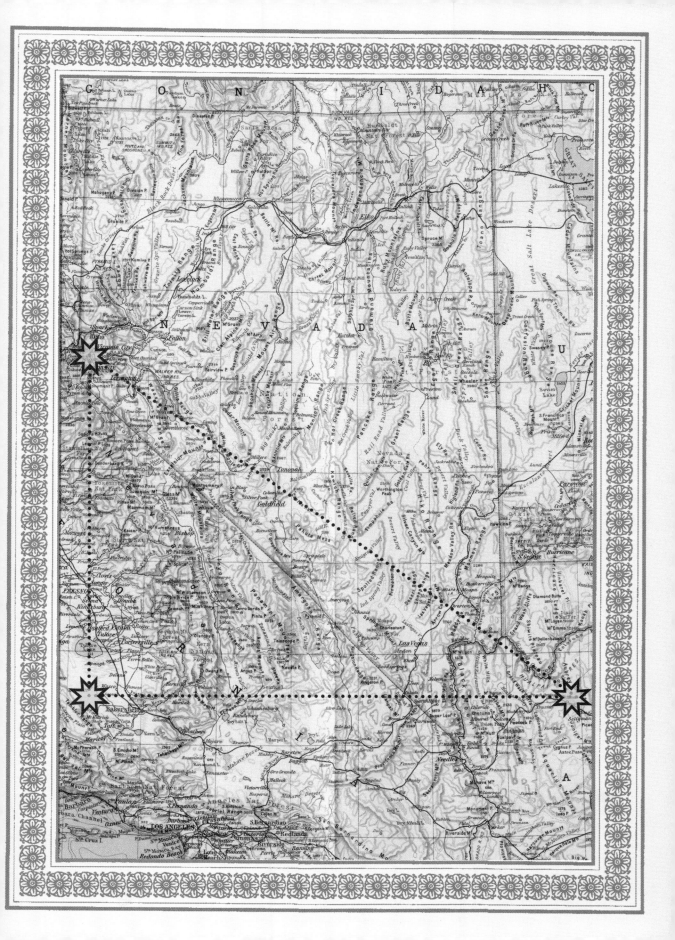

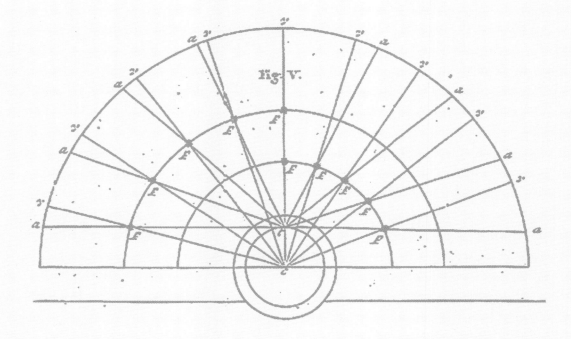

Fig. V.

the middle of the desert, military types being, by nature, very fond of seclusion and wide-open spaces. At 4,687 square miles, the Nellis Air Force Range covers an area thirty times greater than the largest military training site in Europe, and the distance from end to end of the "property" is at least one hundred miles, so there is plenty of scope for getting up to something interesting here. Overflying the range is subject to certain regulations, but at first glance everything seems perfectly transparent. Six airports (three of which are private) are dotted about this vast territory, which is also traversed by a number of extremely quiet roads. At the heart of the "triangle" lies a terra incognita that for more than sixty years has been providing the world's secret services with food for thought while feeding the imaginations of countless ordinary citizens.

Listed in CIA documents as the austere-sounding Area 51, this site, long censored on maps, also possesses a number of more picturesque names, such as Dreamland, Paradise Ranch, Watertown Strip, and Groom Lake (after the dried-up lake that occupies part of the area, known in the nineteenth century mainly for its silver and lead mines). The malevolent reputation of the facility dates back to the postwar years, when atomic bomb trials were being stepped up and President Harry S Truman decided to establish an ultra-secret base here for the testing of all kinds of flying machines and new weapons. Its existence would not be officially acknowledged by the government until it had been going for some forty years. Experimental projects such as the U-2 planes, the Oxcart program, and the astounding Blackbird aircraft were developed

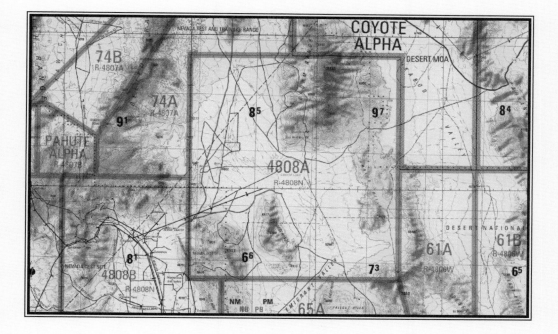

here. But according to some, these sophisticated aircraft are merely the visible tip of a more complicated iceberg. Ufologists all over the planet are passionately interested in this place, their curiosity whetted by the high levels of security surrounding Area 51. If it is impossible to approach the out-of-bounds perimeter without being apprehended by a heavily armed patrol, this is no doubt because unmentionable secrets are being kept here. It is said that concealed beneath the runways is an immense underground base with hangars hollowed out in the mountains surrounding the lake, and even that the facility accommodates a center for extraterrestrial research where the numerous UFOs that have been spotted in the region are held and analyzed—with their crew members, naturally—notably the famous flying saucer that is supposed to have crashed at Roswell, New Mexico, in 1947.

In such an environment, nothing could come as a surprise. The countless disappearances of aircraft in the region? Most probably the result of collisions with spacecraft or nonhomologated deadly weapons, or even the straightforward liquidation of careless intruders by the security services. The real flying enthusiasts, however, do not give such free rein to their imaginations. They know perfectly well that the extreme turbulence generated by this rugged landscape with terrifying thermal variations is effectively a death trap. And they suffer no illusions about the hospitality of this magnificent tomb that is as vast as a small country but more sparsely populated than a village, whose giant sequoias ask no more than to swallow up the imprudent or unlucky hiker forever. Accursed nature strikes again. . . .

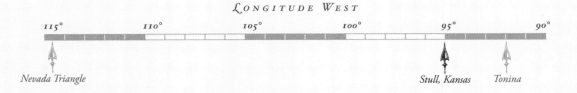
38°58′N – 95°27′W

STULL, KANSAS
THE FORBIDDEN CEMETERY

The gateway to hell is no longer open to visitors. Ever since a particularly eventful Halloween at the end of the 1980s, the police are taking no risks in ensuring that this unassuming little town in Douglas County, in northeastern Kansas, remains just that. Back then the forces of law and order had to remove hundreds of thrill-seekers from Stull Cemetery, where they had gathered to witness manifestations of the devil. The local authorities eventually fenced off the site and put up NO TRESPASSING signs, although that was not enough to deter the most determined. Even now a number of offenders are apprehended and heavily fined every year. The worst times are Halloween and the spring equinox, when the diabolical spirits that haunt these parts are reputed to increase their activity. Large crowds continue to turn up, and television crews looking for scoops are by no means unusual.

Satan must not much care for either the publicity or the police presence, because little is heard of him these days, unlike in the good old days, when nocturnal visitors to the cemetery

Nocturnal visitors to the cemetery would report terrifying accounts of being brushed by invisible creatures.

would report terrifying accounts of being brushed by invisible creatures, thrown to the ground by irresistible forces, and plagued by lugubrious moaning. All this is supposedly explained by a witch buried in the cemetery with whom the devil is supposed to be so enamored that he comes regularly to court her. But no one knows anything about the identity of the mysterious individual. Most conspicuous among the cemetery's residents are the descendants of the first settlers, six farming families of German ancestry who started to work this land in 1857. Two years later, they established a parish, and in 1867 they built the first church in what was then known as Deer Creek Community. At the turn of the century, the village began to be referred to by its current name, which derives from the local postmaster Sylvester Stull. In 1922, a second church was built, the bigger and more practical Stull United Methodist Church, which remains the pride and joy of the active sixty-strong congregation today. The old, abandoned church lies in wrack and ruin, providing a suitable backdrop to the rumors of

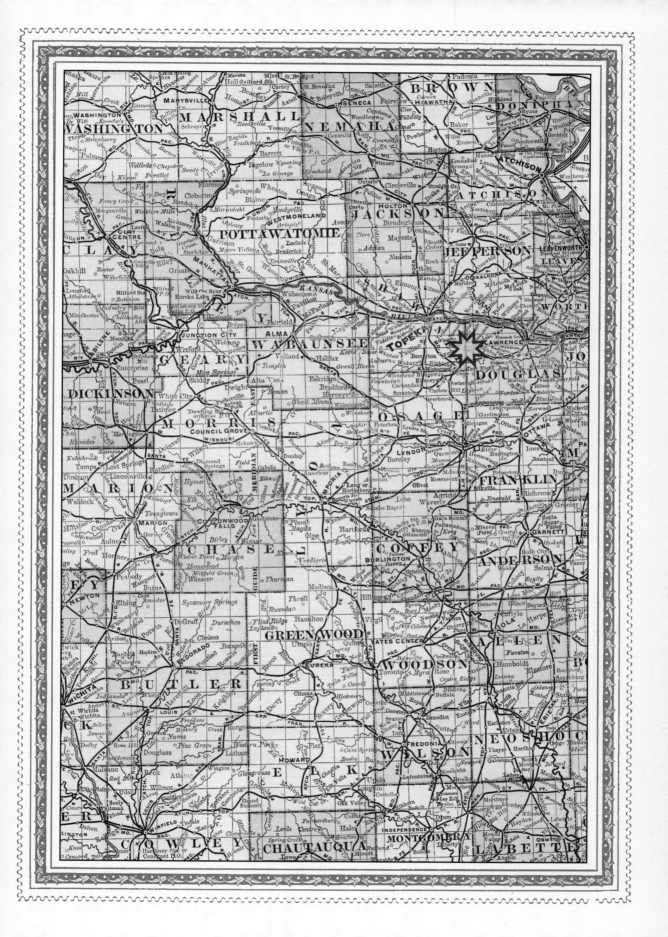

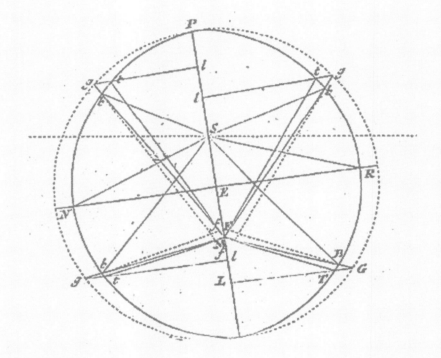

diabolical goings-on that have been insistently spreading since the 1970s.

Student hoax or ancient legend? No one knows anymore. Stull has its share of dark history. At the beginning of the last century a man was found hanging from a tree. A child burned to death in a field fire. And it was not far from this place, in 1854, that the events of Bleeding Kansas were sparked off, setting the state ablaze and contributing to the American Civil War. But that's ancient history. Buffalo no longer graze by Deer Creek, the pine tree that dominated the cemetery for 120 years has been felled, and the old church is no more than a mass of rubble, having been destroyed one night in 2002 by a mechanical digger operated by an anonymous local no doubt driven to the end of his tether—like most of his fellow residents—by the malevolent allure of this ruin.

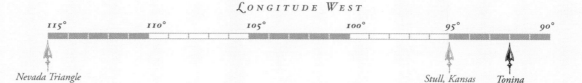
16°54´N – 92°W

TONINA

THE MYSTERY OF THE MAYAS

What calamity could have happened at the dawn of the tenth century to this once influential city that today lies in ruin? The mystery endures, although archeologists are categorical on certain points. It was here, in the present-day state of Chiapas in Mexico, that the last traces of activity of the great Maya civilization have been found and recorded: inscriptions and steles dating back precisely to the year 909. No one is able to say what happened after then. How did this important place, which boasted thirteen temples and eight palaces, and which had shown itself to be more resilient than its prestigious neighbors Palenque, Tikal, and Bonampak, come to be so brutally wiped out?

Between 909 and 1808, the year the remains of the city were comprehensively described for the first time by Guillermo Dupaix, an officer of French origin, on the orders of King Carlos IV of Spain, yawns a gap of nine centuries. For once, the Spanish conquistadors, whose sensitivity to the native populations of Central America is well known, have little to reproach themselves with: By the time they arrived at the beginning of the sixteenth century, Tonina had already been abandoned for a long, long time. It had not

been destroyed, following the deplorable custom beloved of conquering warriors and natural disasters alike, but simply abandoned and then devoured by the equatorial forest. It is as if the inhabitants had decided one fine morning to reject their sacred royalty and the concept of the city-state, hitherto pillars of their political system, and to quit the city without delay in order to start a new life elsewhere. Did the thirty years of drought around the turn of the tenth century diagnosed by scientists for the relevant period have something to do with it? Might the imbalance between demographic development and the deterioration of the arable land lie at the heart of this drama? If so, why would a society this well organized not simply reconstitute itself at a more favorable site?

Perhaps these questions can be answered by contemplating the ancient stones of Tonina, engulfed by greenery a few miles from the city of Ocosingo, or by looking out for anything that can offer an insight into the past, such as the discovery in 2010 of a sarcophagus more than a thousand years old, or by fully appreciating the remarkable thumbing of the nose by this lost civilization— one of the very few in the history of humanity to have confounded generations of researchers.

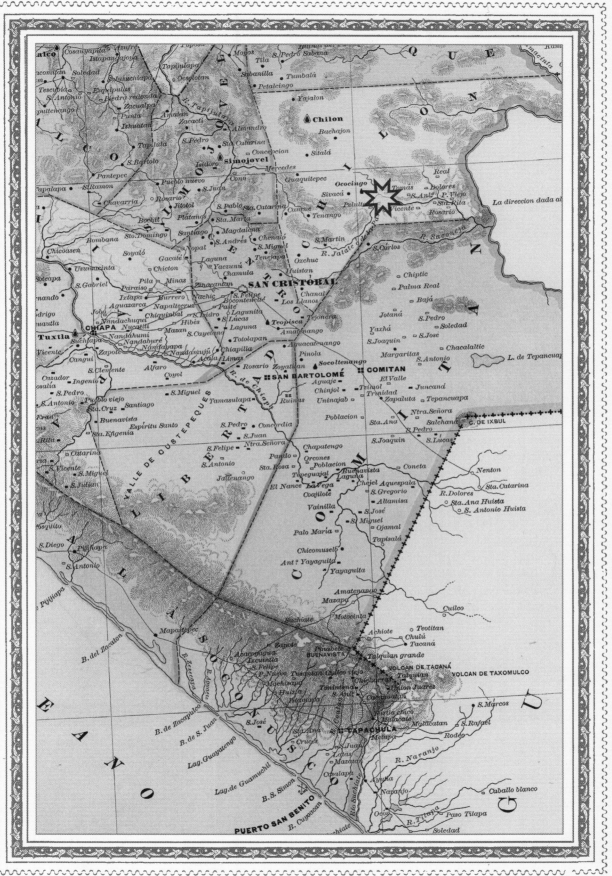

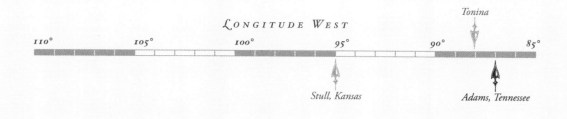

36°35´N – 87°3´W

ADAMS, TENNESSEE
THE BELL WITCH LIVES ON

"I would rather face the full force of the British army than confront the Bell Witch again!" This comment attributed to Andrew Jackson, the seventh president of the United States, testifies to the extraordinary renown achieved by events in the early nineteenth century in a small town in Tennessee that continue to defy logic to this day. Legend has it that prior to being elected president, Jackson, intrigued by the accounts coming out of the town of Adams, went to see for himself, and witnessed the wagon that was carrying him and his staff officers being blocked by a mysterious force. The travelers were then violently cursed by a voice that came out of nowhere. The official biographies of the president do not agree about the report, but Jackson did indeed travel on a regular basis to this part of Robertson County. He may have been aware of a local family that experienced nothing short of a nightmare on the shores of Red River between the years 1817 and 1821.

The haunting began in a relatively low-key way for the farmer John Bell; his wife, Lucy; and their six children, who had lived in this fertile region since 1804. Strange animals were sighted around the farm and unusual noises were heard, discreet at first but gradually more and more obtrusive as the weeks wore on. Within a few months, the situation had become intolerable. The house was plagued by a person

or persons unknown banging on the walls every night, while invisible animals devoured bedding and furniture. And then apparently human sounds could be heard in the darkness, as if an old lady were humming a song outside. In despair, John Bell resolved to talk to his neighbors about it, and they came and spent a night in the farm, where they experienced the same pheomena. The voice soon became more present and intelligible, and started to call out to individual members of the family. Other neighbors were invited in to observe the inexplicable happenings. Before long the haunting of the Bell family was being talked about throughout the whole county. Eventually the word spread beyond state borders and attracted the curious in ever greater numbers, eager to see for themselves what was going on in Adams. For the family, the nightmare continued unabated. After having spent a long time tormenting Betsy, one of the daughters of the family, verbally abusing her day and night, the invisible creature turned her hatred on the father, crying out that she was going to kill him. And she was as good as her word. Exhausted and having grown weaker and weaker, John Bell died in 1820 without any doctor being able to work out what was ailing him. The witching continued for another few months, by the end of which the unknown spirit seemed to lose interest in the grief-stricken Bell family . . . but

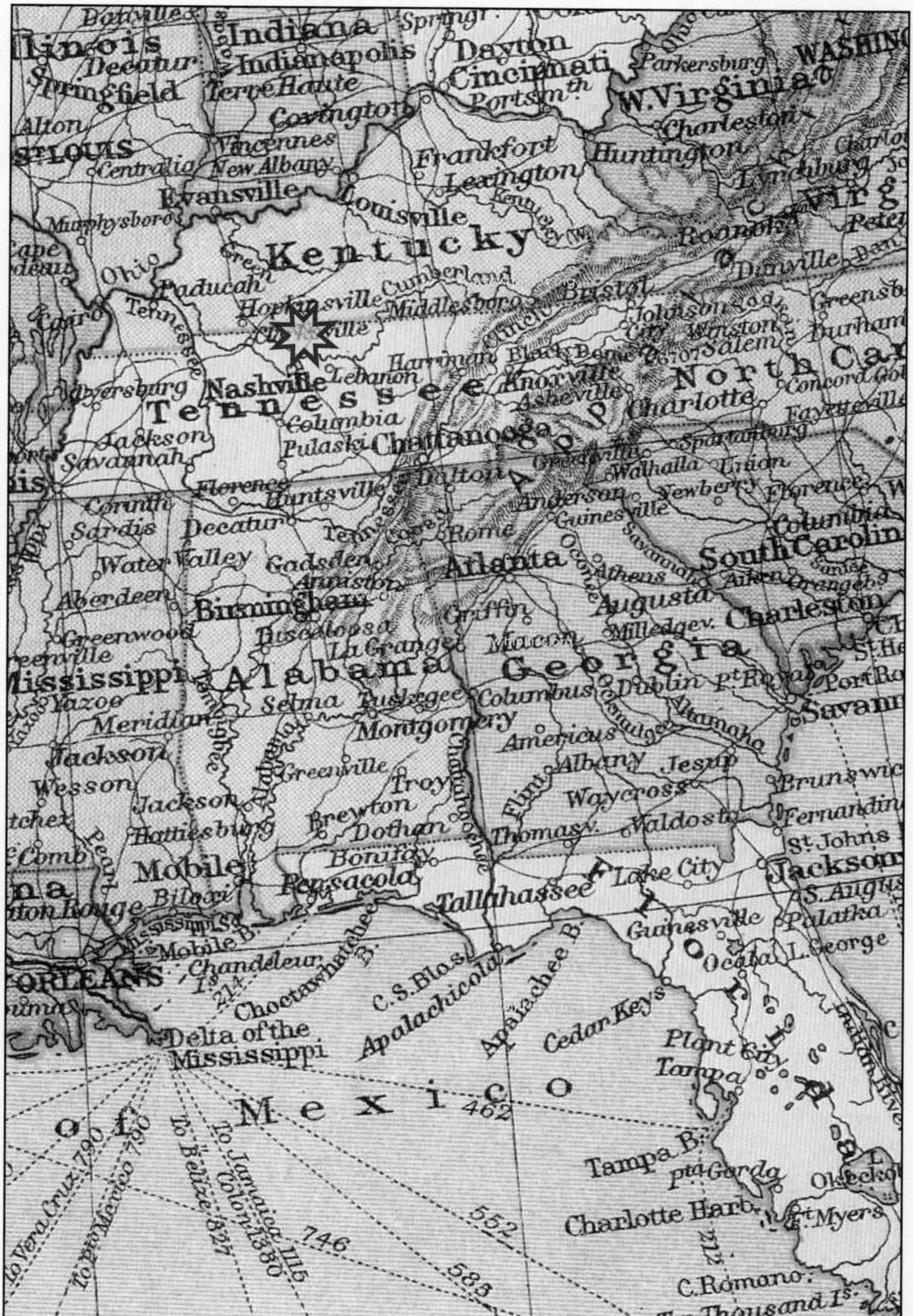

Illinois
Indiana
Indianapolis
Decatur
Springfield
Terre Haute
Dayton
Cincinnati
Portsmth
Parkersburg
W. Virginia
Charleston
Alton
St. Louis
Centralia
Vincennes
New Albany
Covington
Frankfort
Lexington
Huntington
Lynchburg
Evansville
Louisville
Murphysboro
Kentucky
Roanoke
Danville
Ohio
Paducah
Green
Cumberland
Bristol
Cairo
Tennessee
Hopkinsville
Middlesboro
Johnson City
Winston Salem
Greensboro
Durham
Harriman
Knoxville
North Car
Lebanon
Nashville
Asheville
Charlotte
Concord
Dyersburg
Tennessee
Columbia
Fayetteville
Jackson
Pulaski
Chattanooga
Savannah
Spartanburg
Dalton
Walhalla
Union
Florence
Huntsville
Anderson
Newberry
Corinth
Rome
Gainesville
Columbia
Sardis
Decatur
South Carolina
Water Valley
Gadsden
Atlanta
Athens
Aiken
Anniston
Augusta
Orangeb
Aberdeen
Birmingham
Griffin
Charleston
Greenwood
Tuscaloosa
Milledgev.
Greenville
La Grange
Macon
Georgia
Mississippi
Alabama
Dublin
Pt Royal
Yazoo
Selma
Tuskegee
Columbus
Port Royal
Meridian
Montgomery
Savannah
Americus
Jackson
Greenville
Albany
Jesup
Wesson
Troy
Waycross
Brunswick
Jackson
Brewton
Flint
Dothan
Thomasv.
Valdosta
Fernandina
Hattiesburg
Bonifay
St. Johns
Mobile
Pensacola
Lake City
Jacksonville
Biloxi
Tallahassee
S. Augustine
Baton Rouge
Gainesville
Palatka
Mobile B.
L. George
Chandeleur Is
Choctawhatchee B.
C. S. Blas
Apalachicola
Apalachee B.
Ocala
New Orleans
Cedar Keys
Delta of the Mississippi
Plant City
Tampa
of Mexico
462
To Vera Cruz 790
To Mexico 790
To Belize 827
To Jamaica 1115
Colon 1380
Tampa B.
Pta Gorda
Charlotte Harb.
Ft Myers
552
746
583
C. Romano
Ten Thousand Is.
C. Sable

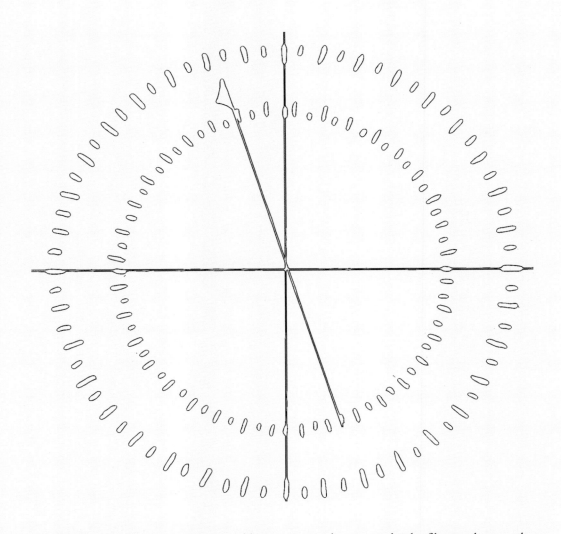

not without first announcing that it would one day return! The locals got into the habit of referring to the spirit as Kate, the name of an old lady who had died shortly before the incidents began. But in reality no one has been able to establish the slightest link between the deceased woman, John Bell, and the presumed witch. One thing is for sure: The latter has lost none of her potency.

To this day visitors flock from all over North America to see where the haunting took place. The current owner of the site preserves the memory of the events and charges visitors some eighteen dollars to view a replica of the farm, the Adams municipality organizes the Bell Witch Bluegrass Festival each year, and the story has

inspired numerous books, films, and even a play performed on site by the Tennessee Theater Company.

Ancient history? Not so fast! Eyewitness accounts of strange goings-on continue to proliferate to this day, including that of the film director Ric White. While location hunting for his movie *The Bell Witch Haunting*, White was astonished to hear his name being aggressively called out by a female voice, without being able to see a living creature anywhere near him. Later, a completely inexplicable fire destroyed his studio and forced him to finish the editing at his home, where, as if by chance, all his equipment started running backward, delaying the release of the movie even further.

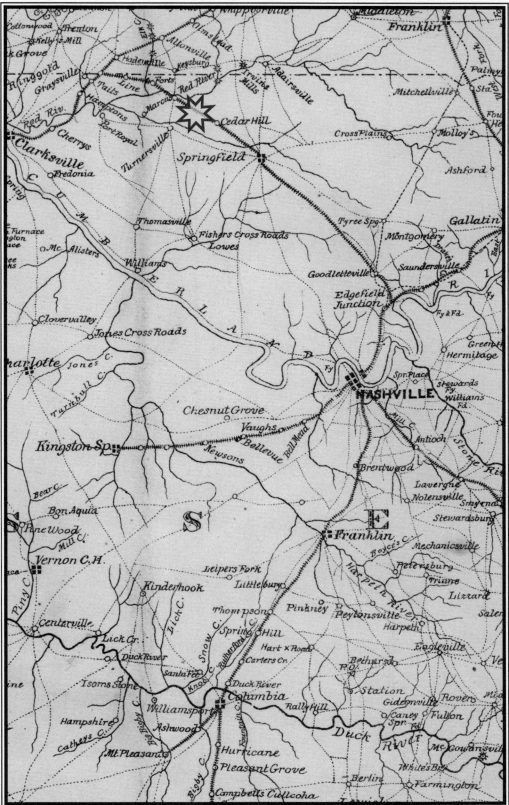

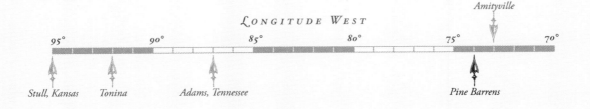
39°45′N – 74°45′W

PINE BARRENS
THE DEVIL'S OFFSPRING

He's here. For more than two centuries, no one has had any doubt of it. The hundreds of witnesses who have had the shock of their lives upon encountering him among the famous pine trees of Wharton State Forest or in the swampland bordering the Mullica River cannot all have been dreaming. But who or what is he? A mutant animal? A monstrous giant bat? An aberrant survivor of the prehistoric pterodactyl? Or, as legend would have it, nothing other than the devil's offspring?

Everyone in these parts is familiar with the story of Deborah Leeds, a mother of twelve children who was reckless enough to curse the heavens upon learning that she was pregnant with her thirteenth. And by all accounts it was a most peculiar child she brought into the world one night in 1735—deformed and malevolent to the point, it is claimed, of killing the midwife who had been summoned to help with the birth. It is then supposed to have disappeared into the labyrinth of forest and water surrounding the shack of Deborah and her husband, Japhet, forever to haunt this corner of the world known since that time as Leeds Point.

a hybrid creature with a winged body, the head of a horse, and the legs and hooves of a goat . . . announcing its presence with a blood-curdling cry

The growth of the surrounding towns and cities over the decades has, it seems, changed nothing. Today the population of New Jersey is one hundred times what it was in the day of the unhappy "Mother Leeds," but despite the proximity of the bright lights of Atlantic City just a dozen miles to the south, the Jersey Devil continues to make this place his own and to get himself talked about—and not only because he inspired the name of the local hockey team. There is no lack of tranquility in this region of spectacular contrasts: At the heart of South Jersey, less than a hundred miles from the megalopolis of New York, the Pineland National Reserve, which covers more than a million acres—22 percent of the total surface area of the state—protects an improbable green expanse in which untamed nature survives in all its glory. Bald eagles and timber rattlesnakes may be at home here, but they do not top the bill any more than the fictional mafioso Soprano family, which set one of the show's bloody episodes here.

The identity of the real master of these parts may be uncertain, but it is of him that hikers think when they stray off the beaten track—and

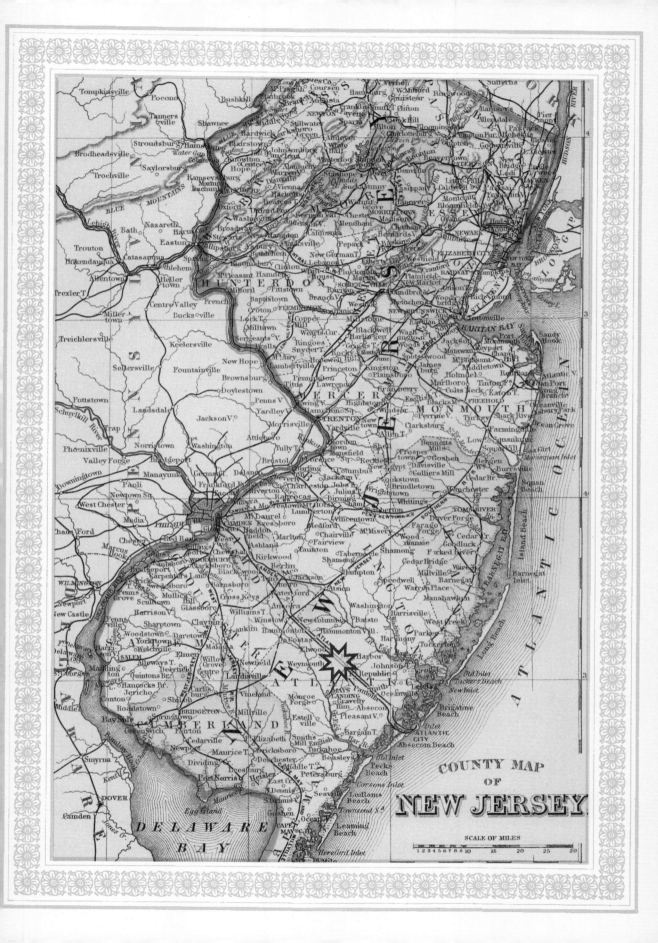

COUNTY MAP
OF
NEW JERSEY

SCALE OF MILES
1 2 3 4 5 6 7 8 9 10   15   20   25   30

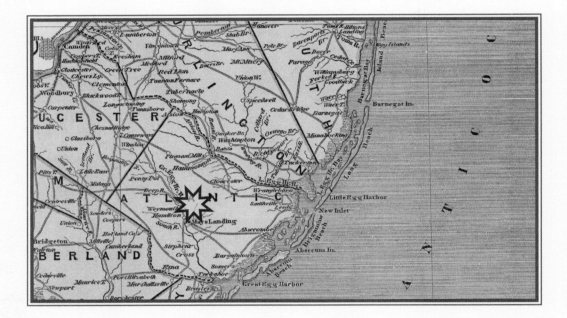

not only when walking the swampy shores of Great Bay, the vast lagoon that separates Pineland Reserve from the Atlantic Ocean, for history shows that the Jersey Devil likes to manifest himself all over his vast territory. He has been spotted near Mystic Island, the bizarre lakeside village surrounded by dense greenery, but also at the gates of Camden, the neighbor of Philadelphia, and even at the northern limits of the forest, which is where Joseph Bonaparte, the older brother of Emperor Napoleon, claimed to have tried in vain to bring him down during a hunting trip in 1820. In 1909 the Jersey Devil sowed panic across the entire state. That year the press published endless witness accounts of citizens who had encountered a hybrid creature with a winged body, the head of a horse, and the legs and hooves of a goat that appeared out of nowhere, rearing high above the heads of mere mortals and announcing its presence with a blood-curdling cry. Such was the alarm that for a while schools remained closed and the inhabitants of various isolated hamlets refused to leave their homes, even to go to work.

Although the mood has calmed down since then, the sightings have not stopped. In 1990 an association was even set up to collect and collate information on the phenomenon, evaluate reports, and try to understand the apparently inexplicable. Sadly, the only aspect that the Devil hunters can corroborate with any degree of certainty is the persistence of the sightings. As throughout the whole of the previous

century, in the new millennium apparently reliable witnesses continue to run across the winged creature resembling nothing else on Earth. But the key to the mystery remains hidden in the undergrowth. For a while it was suggested that the creature could be nothing more exotic than a sandhill crane. But nobody really believes this. After all, who could confuse this elegant wading bird with the "beast" whose dreadful horselike head and ill-assorted limbs have been described in detail by many a hiker and canoeist? What's more, the crane contents itself with a herbivorous diet, while the Jersey Devil, although apparently never having attacked a human being, is known to cause mayhem in the hen house on a regular basis. *Hypsignathus monstrosus* has also been put forward as a candidate, but like the sandhill crane, the hammer-headed bat is a vegetarian and in any case is indigenous to Africa.

While awaiting the discovery of some hypothetical unrecorded species, we therefore have to content ourselves with the memory of the "devil's child" that so caught the imagination in the eighteenth century. Deborah and Japhet Leeds really did live here, and it seems that their thirteenth child indeed led a tragic life.

But it's possible that the story goes back a lot farther, well before the trials and tribulations of Mother Leeds. After all, didn't the Delaware tribe of Native Americans, the very first occupants of this region, name the place Popuessing, meaning "dragon's lair"?

40°40′N – 73°24′W

AMITYVILLE

THE DEVIL'S LAIR

The address can cause some confusion, as 112 Ocean Avenue is in a pretty little residential neighborhood, a good four miles from the Atlantic waves and just twenty minutes by car from JFK, New York's largest airport. The only reminder that this place is connected to the open sea via a vast lagoon that borders a good section of the southern shore of Long Island is the stretch of murky water—160 feet or so wide—just behind the house. This fine building in the colonial style, built in 1924, also possesses a large and functional boathouse on the banks of the creek. This was the main reason that George and Kathy Lutz decided to buy this property in 1975, even though it was actually too expensive for them and, what's more, burdened with a disturbing past. As the owners of a boat, they found the location not only charming but convenient, and they were counting on saving the cost of a berth in the local marina.

Like virtually everyone else in the country, they were familiar with the awful drama that had unfolded within those walls just one year before. During the night of November 13, 1974, Ronald DeFeo Jr. had killed his parents and his four siblings, explaining in his defense that a voice emanating from the house had told him to do it. These mysterious commands were not enough to spare him life imprisonment,

and Mr. and Mrs. Lutz paid no more attention to them than they did to the rumors that this area had been used in the previous century by the native Montaukett people as a burial site. Or to the unknown voice coming from an apparently empty room that hurled the command "Get out!" at the priest who had come to bless the house when its new occupants moved in. The clergyman's response was simply to advise them not to spend too much time in that room.

Having arrived at 112 Ocean Avenue on December 18, 1975, the Lutz family (George, Kathy, and Kathy's three children) left the house in a hurry in January. They claimed to have lived through twenty-eight days of hell there, to have been terrorized by strange goings-on, such as the noise of steps more or less everywhere, music in the cellar, swarms of flies, voices emanating from nowhere, foul smells being given off for no reason, walls oozing heavens knows what, the sensation of invisible creatures brushing up against them, and, to cap it all, the aging of Kathy's face by thirty years in a single night.

No one other than those involved can possibly know what really happened during those four weeks, but people all over the planet would learn about the tiniest details—and more—thanks to the talent of author Jay Anson, who got to know George Lutz and published *The Amityville Horror: A True Story* in 1977. The

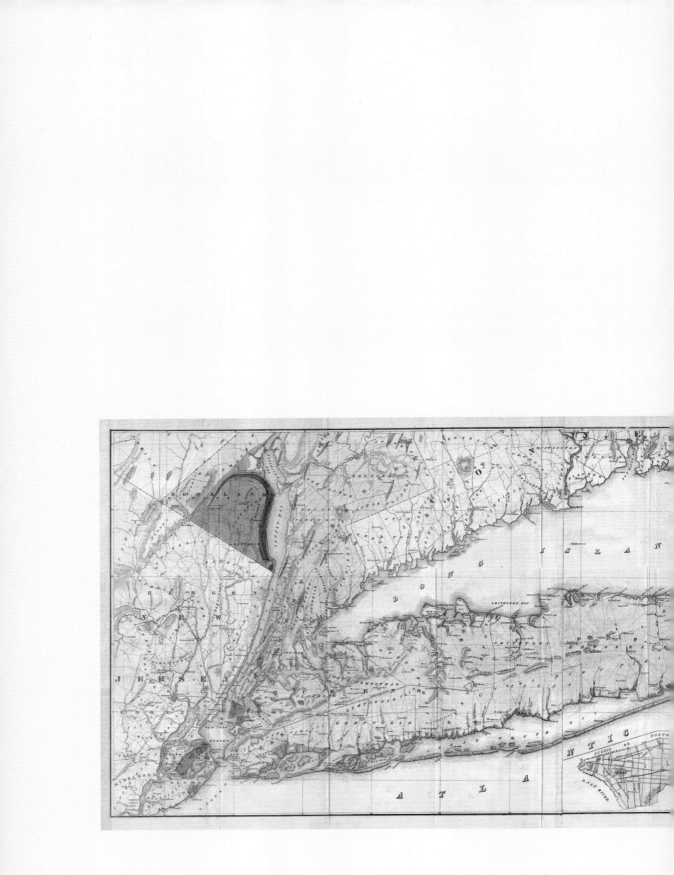

"true story" is clearly embroidered, but it succeeded in terrifying several million readers, and two years later inspired a film of the same name whose special effects were far more spectacular and explicit than the relatively subtle phenomena described by the family.

More malicious commentators suspected George and Kathy of having invented everything in the hope of making money. It is certainly true that the rights to the book and film earned them hundreds of thousands of dollars, but could they have known, when they quit their home, that this story of a haunted house would become an international bestseller? Both died—of natural causes—in the early 2000s. Their eldest son, Daniel, took part in a documentary on the subject at the beginning of 2013. In it he speaks of his father's obsessive interest in occult phenomena and inadvertently raises doubts about his own memory, at times apparently referring to scenes in the film rather than to what he actually experienced as a boy of ten. The house—the real one, rather than the film reconstruction, which is located in Toms River in New Jersey, seventy-five miles away from Amityville—still stands, and if it is indeed cursed, its next owners had no doubt that the book and the movie did the most harm. They had no reason to complain about any abnormal goings-on; on the contrary, they were very happy with their comfortable and attractive home. However, they could have done without the crowds of onlookers coming by in the tens of thousands each year to take a look at the "house of the devil," a public so enthusiastic that it became necessary to change address for a while and erect a fence and plant trees in order to thwart the curious. In the end they even altered the front of the house and gave up the legendary rounded second-floor windows resembling the devil's eyes.

CANADA

NOVA SCOTIA

Winnipeg
Rocky
Missouri
L. Superior
Lake Montreal St. John
Lake Huron
Michigan
Lake: Boston
Lake Ontario Cape Cod
Lake Erie
New York
Philadelphia
Washington
AMERICA
UNITED
Denver
R. Platte
Cincinnati Cape Hatteras
St. Louis
STATES
Mississippi
Red R.
Santa Fe
Mobile
Charleston
Savannah
New Orleans
Rio Grande
Mountains
MEXICO
Guaymas
Cape Canaveral
BAHAMA
ISLANDS
Abaco
San Salvador
Cinaloa
Lucas
Durango
Gulf of Mexico
Santander Havanna
Tampico
Merida
CUBA
Caycos
WEST INDIES
SAN DOMINGO
Porto Rico
Barbuda
Guadaloupe
Dominica
Martinique
Barbadoes
Socoro
Guadalaxara
Mexico
Vera Cruz
Acapulco
Yucatan
Balize Jamaica
Tchuantepec
Leon
CENTRAL
AMERICA
Guatemala
Nicoya
Cartagena
Maracaybo
Curacao
Caribbees Is.
Trinidad
Panama
Varmos
Bogota
Caraccas
R. Orinoco
Georgetown
R. Surinam
Cayenne
Oyopock
GUYANA
VENEZUELA
Cocos Island
Panama Bay
Popayan
NEW
GRENADA
San Fernando
San Carlos
River Amazon
River Para
Atacames
Yapura
River Negro
San Joze
Obidos
Para
Maranh
Galapagos
90
80
Quito
ECUADOR
R.
from Greenwich
100°
110°
Albemarle I.
Guayaquil
Cuenca
Olivenca
San
Madeira
R. Purus
R. Topayos
Kingu
River Tocantins
R. Parnaiba
Oeiras
Alagoas
Sechura
Jaen
R. Beni
SOUTH
Truxillo
Huaro
PERU
B
R. Francisco
Lima
Cuzco
Beira
L. San Anna
Tambo
BOLIVIA
Villa Bella
Villa Boa
Ilh
Pin
Arequipa
Lake Titicaca
Cuyaba
Villa Rica
Bom St
Arica
Chuquisaca
San João del Rey
N. Coimbro
Atacama
AMERICA
TROPIC OF CAPRICORN
er Island
Sales Island
San Ambroise
San Felix
Salta
San Paulo
Espirit
Cape Fr
C
El Juncal
Coquimbo
Asuncion
Tucuman
Rio Janeiro
Juan Fernandez
Valparaiso
Cordova
Santos
Paranagua
Massafuera
Mendoza
URUGUAY
Lake Patos
Rio Grande
Santiago
Concepcion
Buenos Ayres
Monte Video
Rio de la Plata
Valdivia
Cape Corrientes
Island Chloc
Archipeligo of Chonos
Gulf of
San Antonio
Tres Montes
PATAGONIA
Camarones R.
Gulf of St. George
Wellington I.
N
Strait of Magellan
Hoste Island
Terra
Falkland

ATLANTIC OCEAN
Bermudas
TROPIC OF CANC

AMONG THE ISLANDS OF THE NEW WORLD

CITÉ SOLEIL

✳

CAPE HORN

✳

BERMUDA TRIANGLE

✳

SABLE ISLAND

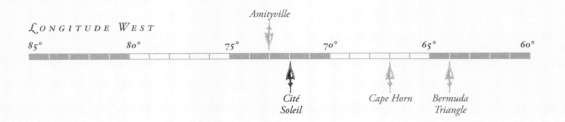
18°34´N – 72°20´W

CITÉ SOLEIL

ALL THE MISFORTUNES ON EARTH

The Haitians don't like to hear it said that their country is plagued by misfortune, and with some justification. Who wouldn't dream of living on an island that is as beautiful as it is fertile; that is washed by a limpid, well-stocked ocean; that basks beneath a sky generous with both sunshine and fresh water? And on top of all this, it is a nation that has nurtured so many artists and writers and in 1804 gave the whole world a lesson in emancipation with the founding, by former rebel slaves, of the first republic with a majority black population.

Haiti is therefore a blessed land, a land that simply has the misfortune of finding itself in the path of the North Atlantic cyclones (the merciless Hurricane Jeanne, for example, which was responsible for two thousand deaths in 2004) and of being a little too susceptible to seismic shocks (the earthquake in January 2010 claimed more than three thousand victims and destroyed a large part of the capital, Port-au-Prince).

Natural disasters affect the neighboring islands as well, of course, but their efforts never have as gratifying an effect there as on the typically somewhat haphazardly constructed Haitian homes—huts made of sheet metal and other scavenged material. This is just the tip of the catastrophically bad luck. Since its moment of glory in 1804, the population has never had a moment of peace. What with punches below the belt delivered by colonial powers, the excessive financial cost of independence from the country's former "guardian," and a complicated political life (from a megalomaniac emperor to corrupt presidents, with the attendant coups d'état) entailing almost continuous violence for two centuries.

So life is not always easy in Haiti. But there are degrees of hardship. For example, it is better to be the owner of a pretty villa on the top of Morne Calvaire than to be a resident of Cité Soleil—a name well chosen, incidentally, as sunshine is the only "service" from which the 250,000 people packed into this shantytown wedged between the sea and the airport benefit. Pools of putrid water, swarms of mosquitos, floods that occur as soon as there's a little too much rain, few working toilets, and omnipresent garbage make life here a curse. In addition, this insalubrious place is prey to gangs, whether serving the political factions or their own interests, who spread terror despite the efforts of the local police and the United Nations.

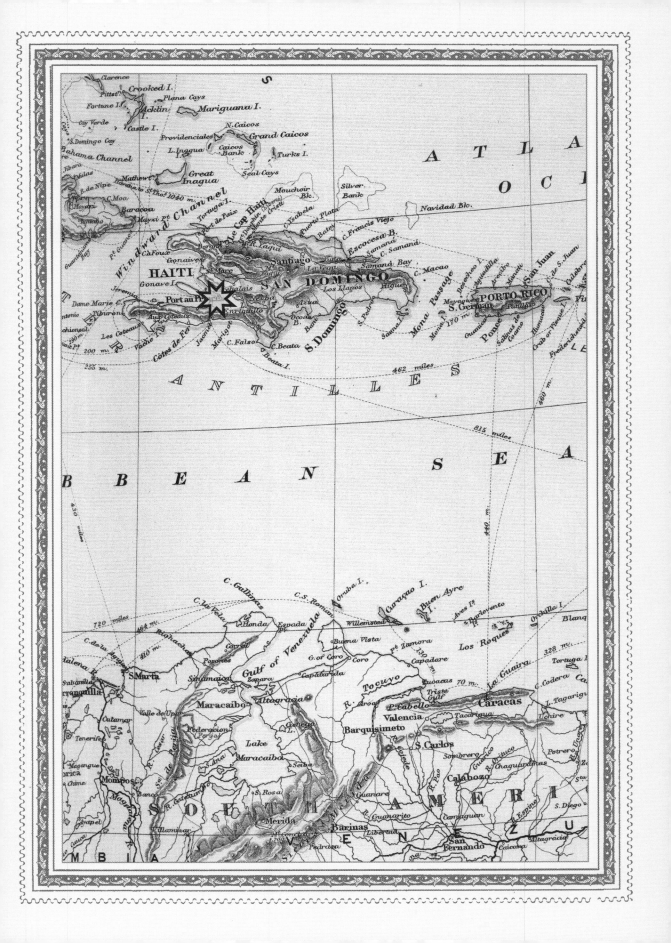

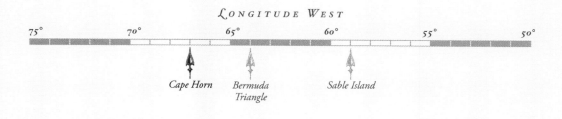
55°58′S – 67°17′W

CAPE HORN
SAILOR'S NIGHTMARE

When approaching this much-feared rock bearing the name of the pleasant Dutch fishing port of Hoorn, it is the statistics that first strike fear into the heart: Eight hundred shipwrecks have been recorded in the vicinity of Cape Horn in less than two centuries, corresponding no doubt to a tally in human lives of an estimated twenty thousand. From closer range, it is the hostile environment that makes the blood run cold: gray sea, brooding cliffs, impressive swell, often-poor visibility, rain, strong wind, cold—and always the feeling that one's troubles are only just beginning, that the next squall could be worse than the last.

What were all those unfortunate souls doing in such a cursed place? Quite simply, working. Before the Tierra del Fuego became a sought-after destination among racing yachtsmen and a handful of aesthete-travelers with a hankering for unspoiled landscapes, no one came here unless it was their job. A living had to be earned, and this place was on one of the main commercial routes. In those days it often took almost four months to reach San Francisco from New York, or occasionally less, if travelers were lucky enough to get a passage on as fast a ship as

> *gray sea, brooding cliffs, impressive swell, often poor visibility, rain, strong wind, cold . . .*

the extraordinary *Flying Cloud*, which in 1853 attained a record journey time of eighty-nine days.

It's a safe bet that more than one Cape Horner has cursed geography—in particular the impenetrable logic of the continents whereby America descends twenty or so degrees farther south in latitude than Africa. If rounding the Cape of Good Hope was not always a picnic (it was initially baptized the Cape of Storms), what can be said of Cape Horn, located a further 1,500 miles south, close to the icy wastes of the Antarctic? Separating the two are at least fifteen degrees in temperature and a long voyage filled with trials and tribulations. Sailors have to suffer the violent, gusting wind that hurtles down from the Andes, tame the sinister Roaring Forties, and tackle the Furious Fifties. The cyclones follow in quick succession, and the sea becomes a monster, as there's nothing more to bar its way. Driven by the big westerly winds, the swell does a tour of the earth, growing ever bigger as it pursues its crazy course. And it's even worse at the level of Cape Horn itself, with the brutal upwelling onto the continental shelf, causing the waves to grow even larger and rendering the ocean still more chaotic, not to mention the acceleration of the wind as soon as it surges into

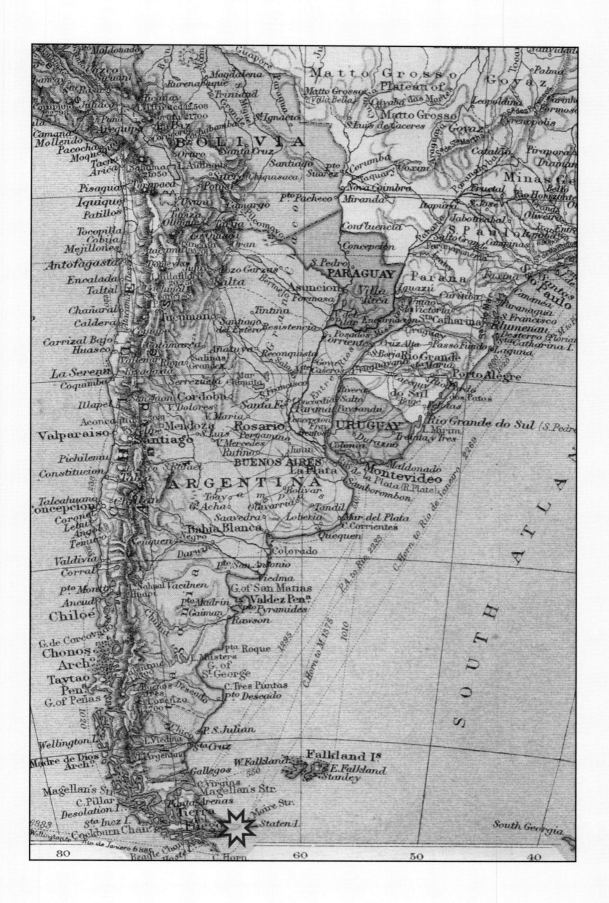

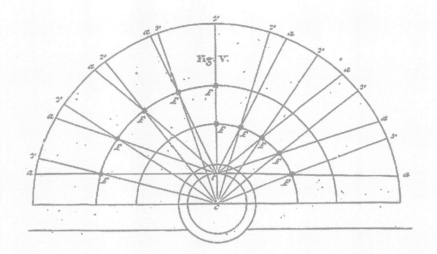

Drake Passage between the land masses of America and Antarctica, which channel its path.

Sailors used to say that to enter the high latitudes was to abandon the world of humanity. This was a voyage all the more trying because it could drag on, during the heroic days of sailing at least, for an eternity. The main problem when entering the Pacific was that the prevailing winds had to be battled, and sailing ships were ill-suited to this challenge. To journey from the fiftieth parallel on the Atlantic side to the same latitude on the other side could take a whole month or sometimes longer. These would be agonizing weeks spent tacking between Patagonia and the Antarctic Peninsula, making little or no headway as the rigging iced up and the crew suffered unspeakable misery. Some captains would end up throwing in the towel, putting in at a neighboring inlet in the hope that the wind would turn. There are even reports of others heading off in an easterly direction, worn out by the struggle and choosing instead to make for the Pacific via the Atlantic and the Indian Ocean!

In *The Voyage of the Beagle*, Charles Darwin described his journey around the Horn in 1832:

> . . . we closed in with the Barnevelts, and running past Cape Deceit with its stony peaks, about three o'clock doubled the weather-beaten Cape Horn. The evening was calm and bright, and we enjoyed a fine view of the surrounding isles. Cape Horn, however, demanded his tribute, and before night sent us a gale of wind directly in our teeth. We stood out to sea, and on the second day again made the land, when we saw on our weather-bow this notorious promontory in its proper form—veiled in a mist, and its dim outline surrounded by a storm of wind and water. Great black clouds were rolling across the heavens, and squalls of rain, with hail, swept by us with such extreme violence, that the Captain determined to run into Wigwam Cove. This is a snug little harbour, not far from Cape Horn; and here, at Christmas-eve, we anchored in smooth water.

The opening of the Panama Canal in 1914 wiped out much of the interest in this particular maritime route, enabling distances to be drastically reduced (the journey between New York and San Francisco was cut by eight thousand miles) as well as the difficulties of effecting the Atlantic/Pacific transition. Cape Horn got what it deserved, forfeiting most of its "customers" after tormenting them for so long. Its capacity to make a nuisance of itself remains undiminished, however. It simply must confine this activity to those latter-day adventurers who are still fascinated by its legend.

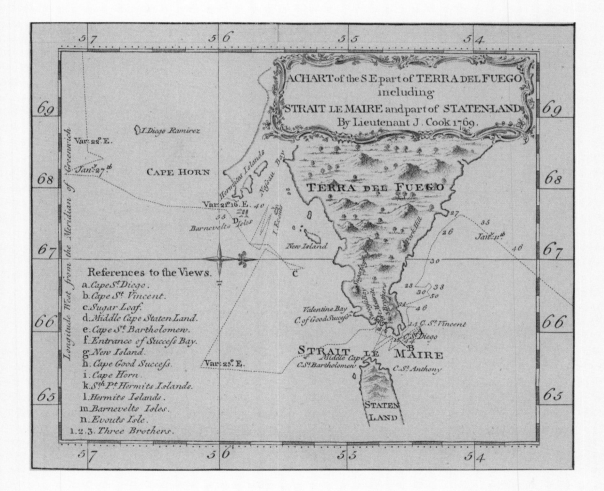

A CHART of the S E part of TERRA DEL FUEGO
including
STRAIT LE MAIRE and part of STATEN-LAND.
By Lieutenant J. Cook 1769.

TERRA DEL FUEGO

CAPE HORN

I. Diego Ramirez

Var.ᵗ 22°. E.

Jan.ᵗ 27ᵗʰ

Var.ᵗ 21°.16.E.

Barnevelts Isles

New Island

Var.ᵗ 25°. E.

Jan.ᵗ 11ᵗʰ

Valentine Bay
C. of Good Success

STRAIT LE MAIRE

Middle Cape
C. Sᵗ. Bartholomew
C. Sᵗ. Anthony
C. Sᵗ. Vincent
C. Sᵗ. Diego

STATEN LAND

Longitude West from the Meridian of Greenwich

References to the Views.
a. Cape Sᵗ. Diego.
b. Cape Sᵗ. Vincent.
c. Sugar Loaf.
d. Middle Cape Staten Land.
e. Cape Sᵗ. Bartholomew.
f. Entrance of Success Bay.
g. New Island.
h. Cape Good Success.
i. Cape Horn.
k. Sᵗʰ Pᵗ Hermits Islands.
l. Hermits Islands.
m. Barnevelts Isles.
n. Evouts Isle.
1.2.3. Three Brothers.

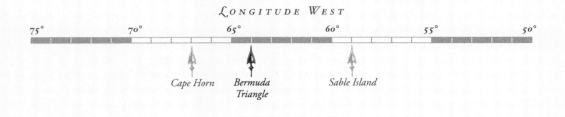
31°17′N – 64°46′W

BERMUDA TRIANGLE

EMPIRE OF ENIGMAS

The more malicious of observers are fond of claiming that what vanishes most quickly in the vicinity of Bermuda is money, this "Little Switzerland of the Atlantic" displaying an astonishing degree of creativity as a tax haven. However, one should never listen to malicious gossip or joke about air and sea disasters. And disasters are something of which this triangle in the sea, wedged between Bermuda, Florida, and Puerto Rico, has had more than its fair share, starting with the enigma of Flight 19, a group of five US Navy fighters that vanished into thin air north of the Bahamas on December 5, 1945. This incident began as a routine training exercise. The TBF Avengers took off from Fort Lauderdale in the early afternoon on a sea bombing exercise. The control tower picked up the final message from the flight leader at 18:04 hours: "Keep strict formation. . . . We're going to have to land on the sea. . . . When the first gauge drops below ten gallons, we'll all descend together." And then nothing. No trace was ever found of either the aircraft or their fourteen crew members. The inquiry established that the planes had flown in a circle for part of the afternoon, clearly lost, before getting low on fuel and attempting a landing. But the tragedy doesn't stop there: A Catalina flying boat was dispatched in the early

evening with thirteen people on board to assist Flight 19. It was never seen again either.

Three years later, two planes with passengers on board disappeared in equally mysterious circumstances: one just before landing on Bermuda, the other on the approach into Miami. Further air accidents occurred over the next few years, and in 1963, the *Sulfur Queen* went missing in the Straits of Florida with thirty-nine sailors on board, increasing the pressure a notch. In February 1964, the American journalist Vincent Gaddis published an article in the popular magazine *Argosy*, describing for the very first time the curse he called the Bermuda Triangle. An attempt was made to compile an inventory of the accidents that have occurred in the zone over the previous decades, yielding a tally of forty-eight aircraft and 190 ships in a century— including the sloop of the celebrated Joshua Slocum, the first man to single-handedly circum-navigate the world in a sailing boat, who disappeared in these environs in November 1909. All sorts of theories have been suggested, ranging from the rational to the far-fetched: a magnetic irregularity that interferes with compasses, a plot by the government or some foreign power, a spatiotemporal hole, extraterrestrial activity, the influence of the mythical lost civilization of Atlantis (which is supposed to have been

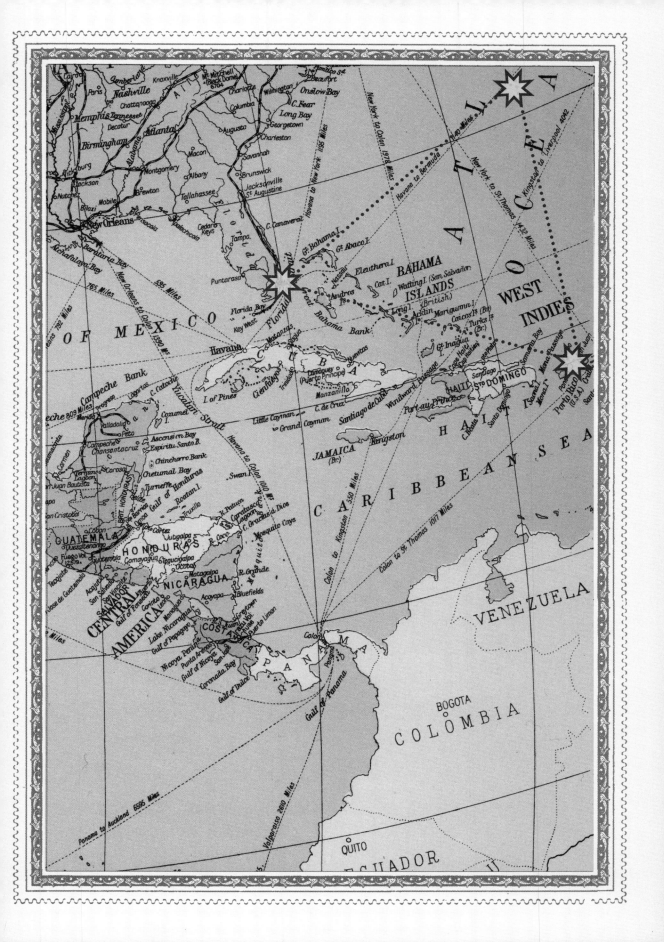

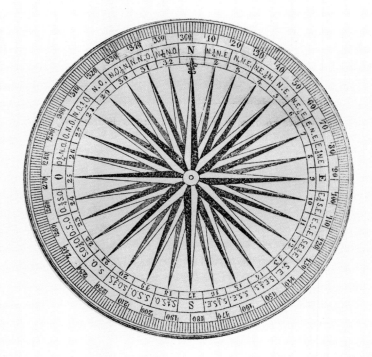

engulfed by the waves at this precise spot). More recently, theories center on the discovery of large quantities of gas hydrates at the bottom of the ocean, which, when they discharge into the sea and then the atmosphere, are said to alter the buoyancy of the water and the lift of the air, causing boats to sink and planes to drop out of the sky without warning.

All the apparently unanswered questions have made at least one man happy: Charles Berlitz, grandson of the founder of the famous language school, who has sold twenty million copies of *The Bermuda Triangle*. His book, published in 1974, purports to explain the role played by paranormal phenomena in these disappearances, but in reality the only intervention by the paranormal is the infatuation stirred up by an affair that is, no doubt, far more trivial than it appears. For it seems that Flight 19 was not the victim of any mysterious force, but simply disappeared as the result of a gross navigational error on the part of its leader, whose attempt to land at night in strong winds and on a raging sea—as was the case on December 5, 1945—

was doomed to failure. Furthermore, according to the investigators, the Catalina flying boat exploded on takeoff, an accident of a type that has occurred throughout the history of aviation, even far from Bermuda. And the *Sulfur Queen*? It was an ancient and poorly maintained tanker with a cargo of liquid sulfur, a vessel considered by the experts of the day to be completely unseaworthy. In all probability, bad weather conditions were not even needed for that particular ship to go down. Even the sad end of the unforgettable Joshua Slocum has a rational explanation. It has to be remembered that this was a man of sixty-five years of age, every bit as tired as his trusty *Spray*—itself more or less a centenarian!—sailing from Bristol to the Antilles, a route that, thanks to classic storms and tropical cyclones, is not without its hazards in the autumn.

While people navigate the area every day without incident, and there are often logical explanations for any incident, the Bermuda Triangle's mystique will always capture the public's imagination.

Catherines P.
The Narrows
Murroy Anchorage
S.t George
& I.
S.t George
Harb.
Smith
Cone I.
Long Bird
S.t David I.
Baileys B.
Castle
Cooper
Crawl Pt.
Castle
Harbour
Nonsuch I.
Charles I.
Dockyard
The Stags
Trunk
Castle P.t
Ireland I.
Shelly B.
Grassy Bay
Tuckers Tn.
Boaz I.
Gallows I.
Chamberlain
B.
Admiralty Ho.
Flats Vill.
Mangrove Co.
Harrington S.d
Daniels
I. &c.a
Spanish P.t
Somerset I.d
Watford I.
Walker B.
Sound
Hamilton
Farris B.
Heydon B.
Elizabeth I.
Hamilton Harb.
Great Barrel I.
Hungry B.
Grace I.
Hogfish Cut
Tucker
Heron
Pt. Royal
Bay
Chaddock
Bay
Great Turtle B.

BERMUDA

Eng. Miles

0   1   2

Roads
Lighthouses

Church D.
Port Royal
Gibbs Hill

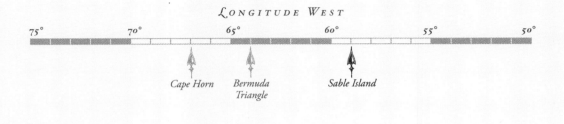

43°55′N – 59°55′W

SABLE ISLAND

A SHIP TRAP IN THE ATLANTIC

Where misfortune is concerned, efficiency sometimes goes hand in hand with unobtrusiveness. Take the example of this long sandbar off Nova Scotia, which, although not remotely enjoying the notoriety of the fabled Bermuda Triangle, has displayed a far greater aptitude for interfering with shipping. Totally unknown to most landlubbers, this island—unpopulated other than for a few passing scientists and several hundred wild horses—can pride itself on having single-handedly destroyed more than 350 vessels since the end of the sixteenth century (and no doubt many others before then that no one took the trouble to count). But thanks to the sand, which over time gently but surely digests her prey, leaving behind only pristine beaches of a reassuring paleness, she is modest in her victory. Here there are no jagged reefs or terrifying whirlpools, just the banality of evil, if one may put it like that: a low-lying and therefore not highly visible tract of land located in the middle of a zone frequented by numerous craft such as cod-fishing boats attracted by the well-stocked fishing grounds of Newfoundland and miscellaneous vessels heading for the Gulf of Saint Lawrence or the port of Halifax, 186 miles west-northwest.

Here there are no jagged reefs or terrifying whirlpools, just the banality of evil.

All it takes is a small navigational error for mariners to discover before their bows—all too late—the rollers of Sable Island rather than the open water they had expected. And this in a region whose dreadful weather is part of the picture—for example, the fog that descends one day out of three, favored by the currents from Labrador and Belle Isle crossing the Gulf Stream. So many boats have been lost here that the Nova Scotia administration eventually decided to take action and in 1801 set up a permanent sea rescue station on the island in order to come to the aid of shipwreck victims. This was followed in 1872, a little after the terrible shipwreck of the liner SS *Hungarian* (single-handedly responsible for 330 victims) by the installation of new lighthouses in order to make it easier for sailors to get their bearings in the shallows.

The spread of satellite navigation systems at the end of the twentieth century badly affected the notoriety of the island, which can now only count on the inept to garnish its beaches. And in the future it may well get a taste of its own medicine: Having become a Canadian national park, this beautiful loner will perhaps, instead, be subjected to the indignities of disrespectful tourists.

N

W   E

BENEATH THE ATLANTIC BREEZE

CUMBRE VIEJA

✳

EILEAN MOR

✳

YEUN ELLEZ

✳

TIFFAUGES

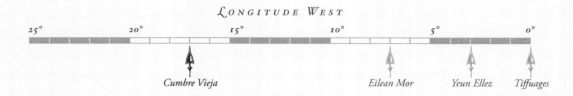
28°34´N – 17°50´W

CUMBRE VIEJA
BIRTHPLACE OF THE TSUNAMI

Don't be fooled by appearances: It is perfectly possible for a topographical feature to have a name that translates as "old summit" yet display a degree of vitality that strikes fear into the hearts of its immediate neighbors, and those of others, too. This volcano rises proudly to a height of more than a mile on the island of La Palma in the Canaries. It offers the double disadvantage of retaining plenty of potential for volcanic activity while at the same time suffering from a certain fragility that could transform any future eruption into a catastrophe affecting not only the archipelago itself, but also the American, African, and European mainlands.

This is due to the instability of the mountain's western flank, which specialists claim could collapse into the sea in the event of a shock. This would most likely result in a monumental tsunami that would affect most of the countries bordering the Atlantic.

It's a simple question of numbers: 650,000 cubic yards of rock (a high estimate) could crash into the ocean, producing an enormous displacement of water that within a few minutes would result in the emergence of an enormous dome of liquid several hundred yards higher than normal sea level. The resulting wave would set off across the ocean in every direction at more than 425 miles an hour. Ten minutes after the collapse, the neighboring islands of Hierro and La Gomera would be swamped by monstrous tidal waves. After an hour, the Moroccan coast would in turn be hit by waves hundreds of feet high. Europe would be relatively unaffected, although southwest-facing parts of Brittany, England, and Ireland would suffer damage, as would the western tip of Spain. Six hours after the start of operations, the tsunami would attack the coast of Brazil, the Antilles, and Saint Pierre and Miquelon. Three hours later it would reach the United States, notably Florida, which would find itself under water and pounded by waves sixty-five feet high.

There is nevertheless one piece of good news: Scientists are divided on the reliability of the modeling tools employed, and the tsunami could be less powerful than anticipated.

> *The resulting wave would set off across the ocean in every direction at more than 425 miles an hour.*

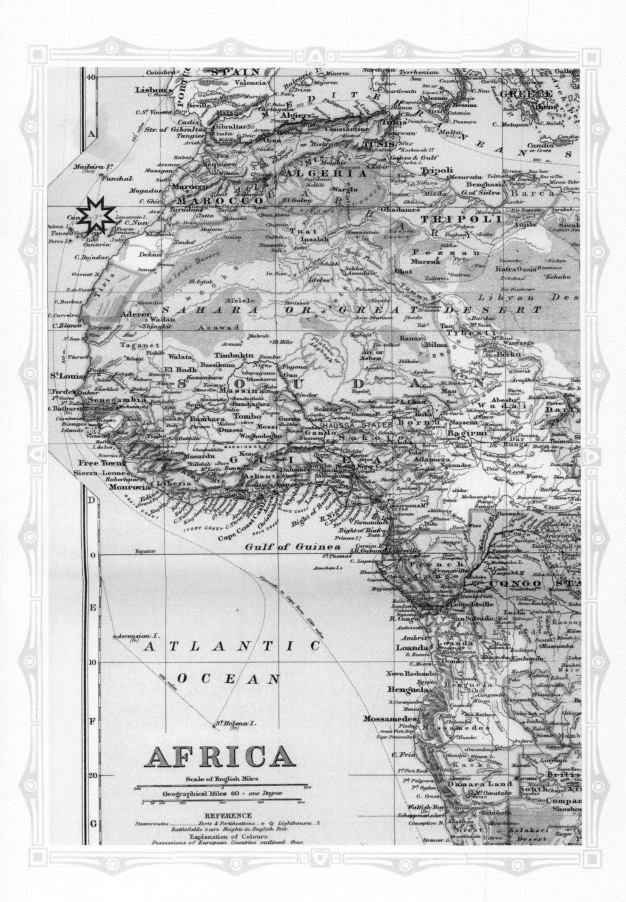

AFRICA

Scale of English Miles

Geographical Miles 60 = one Degree

REFERENCE

Steamroutes.......... Forts & Fortifications ✠ ✩ Lighthouses ⚲
Battlefields ⚔ Heights in English Feet.

Explanation of Colours.
Possessions of European Countries outlined thus.

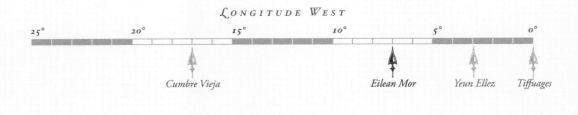
58°17′N – 7°35′W

EILEAN MOR

LIGHTHOUSE MYSTERY

This superb lighthouse, completed in 1899, was built to warn sailors of the dangers of the small but hazardous Flannan Isles, off the Outer Hebrides. Alas, barely a year later, the lighthouse became the scene of one of the most perplexing island mysteries in history.

On December 15, 1900, the steamboat *Archtor*, sailing from Philadelphia to Leith, the port of Edinburgh, almost ran aground on the Flannan Isles for the simple and inexplicable reason that the Eilean Mor lighthouse was not lit. As soon as the vessel reached its destination, its commanding officer notified the authorities, but it was not until December 26 that the *Hesperus*, the Hebrides service boat, was able to get to the island and ascertain that something out of the ordinary had clearly occurred there. The lantern was still extinguished, the regulation flag was not flying and, most importantly, there was nobody about, raising the question: What had happened to the three keepers? There was only one oilskin hanging in the closet, which seemed to indicate that the three men had gone out in their wet-weather gear. But where? It was impossible to walk for more than a hundred yards in any direction, and they had no boat on which to leave the island. And why would the third keeper have left his oilskin behind to go out onto the cold and humid rock in the middle of December? Had they been carried off while working on the slipway by a wave they had not seen coming? Yet, the sea had been calm throughout the middle of the month.

Reading the lighthouse logbook plunged the *Hesperus* crew, and subsequently the investigators, into even greater bewilderment. On the page for December 12, Thomas Marshall, the first assistant, had recorded "severe winds the like of which I have never seen before in twenty years." He also mentions that James Ducat—the chief keeper—remained "very quiet," while William McArthur—the second assistant—had wept. On December 13, he noted that the storm was still raging and that the three men had begun to pray. Why would the Scottish mariners, all experienced men noted for their bravery, have cried and prayed when they were safe and sound in a newly built lighthouse perched more than thirty yards above the sea? And there's worse: All the observations made by ships and land stations in the region confirm that the weather had been fine between December 12 and 15, without the slightest storm.

Some of the keepers who subsequently took over the lighthouse claimed to have heard strange noises at night when the wind was howling around the rock. But a lot of strange things can be heard in an isolated lighthouse in the middle of the ocean, six hours by boat from the nearest village. No clue and no satisfactory explanation of the Eilean Mor mystery has been found in more than a century. This leaves just the final entry in the log, dated December 15, 1900: "God is over all." Indeed, but surely there's something else?

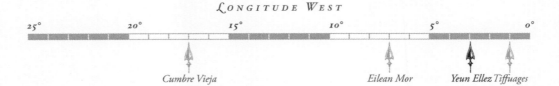

48°21′N – 3°53′W

YEUN ELLEZ
THE MARSH OF THE DAMNED

An abandoned nuclear power station, a marsh that leads straight down to hell, a river o'erflown by angels . . . here the magic of the past takes a sly pleasure in interweaving with that of the present. The river of angels is the Ellez, whose course is followed by the winged creatures who come to free the captive souls of the dead and open up the gates of purgatory for them. But, more accurately, this should be in the past tense because it is not known what route the angels take now that the Nestavel dam and the 1937 flooding of this extraordinary natural basin in the Monts d'Arrée have interfered with the river's course. As a result, several dozen hectares of *yeun*—Breton for *marshland*—disappeared beneath the water and with them a substantial part of the peat bogs that were one of the rare jewels of these desolate landscapes.

Did this artificial reservoir, used until 1967 to cool down the Brennilis power station, at the same time quell the legendary *youdig*, the heart of the marsh that was said to be bottomless? We would be prepared to bet that the Arrée peasants of yore, who trembled as they kept an eye out for Ankou, that devoted servant of Death who marked the next unfortunate souls to be called to their maker, would have seen the unfathomable *youdig*, reputed to be a gateway to hell, as nothing but a nuisance, and fretted about what it might conceal.

Exorcist priests are said to have led the damned into the marsh after transforming them into black dogs. Thanks to folklorist Anatole Le Braz, it is even known with some degree of precision how this occurred. In 1893, the Breton writer made a methodical compilation of various choice writings on the subject, such as this one describing how the devil's henchmen were rendered unto their master: "As soon as they have been cast in, one must lie flat on one's stomach and place one's hands firmly over one's ears, because the entrails of the marsh will be seized by a tremendous shaking and horrible clamors will rent the air. Before making one's way home, it is important to wait until the sabbath has come to an end. And then one should run away as quickly as possible, taking care not to turn one's head. Woe betide anyone who disobeys this rule, for invisible arms will attach themselves to that person and drag him into the hidden depths."

And then of course there were everyday accidents. In certain places the ground is so swampy that lost walkers could, it seems, disappear without trace. Ankou may not be mentioned quite so often here today, but this character inherited from Celtic mythology has certainly not disappeared, and can still be seen adorning various Christian edifices. And Druid ceremonies are performed on the shores of the reservoir, perhaps keeping him at bay.

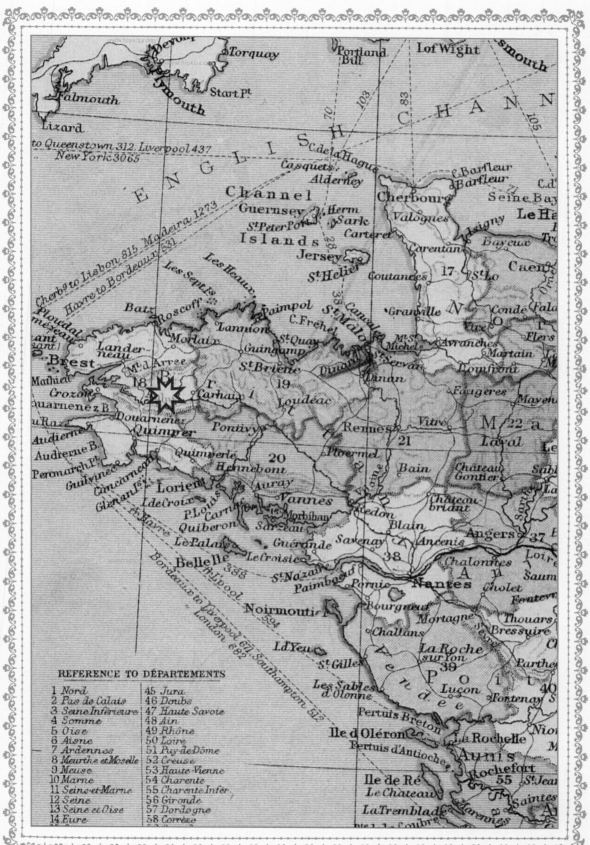

ENGLISH CHANNEL

Torquay
Portland Bill
I. of Wight
Plymouth
Start Pt.
Falmouth
Lizard
to Queenstown 312. Liverpool 437
New York 3065
C. de la Hague
Casquets
Alderney
Channel
Guernsey
Herm
St. Peter Port
Sark
Carteret
Islands
Jersey
St. Helier
Coutances
C. Barfleur
Barfleur
Cherbourg
Valognes
Seine Bay
Le Havre
Isigny
Bayeux
Carentan
Caen
17
St. Lo
Granville
N
Condé
Falaise
Vire
Flers
Avranches
Mortain
Domfront
Fougères
Mayenne
Havre to Bordeaux 631
Madeira 1273
Les Heaux
Les Sept Is.
Batz
Roscoff
Paimpol
C. Fréhel
St. Malo
Ploudal
méreau
Morlaix
Lannion
Guingamp
St. Quay
St. Servan
Dinard
Dinan
Mt. St. Michel
Landerneau
St. Brieuc
19
Loudéac
Vitré
M
22
Brest
Mt. d'Arrée
Carhaix
Rennes
21
Laval
Mathieu
Crozon
Douarnenez B.
Quimper
Pontivy
Ploermel
Bain
Château Gontier
u Raz
Audierne
Audierne B.
Quimperle
20
Hennebont
Auray
Vannes
Redon
Blain
Châteaubriant
Penmarch Pt.
Guilvinec
Concarneau
Lorient
I. de Croix
P. Louis
Carn
Morbihan
Sarzeau
Savenay
Ancenis
Angers
37
Glenan Is.
Quiberon
Le Palais
Guérande
Blain
Chalonnes
Saumur
Belle I.
St. Nazaire
Paimbœuf
Pornic
Nantes
Cholet
Fontevr.
Noirmoutier
Bourgneuf
Mortagne
Thouars
Bressuire
Challans
St. Gilles
Les Sables d'Olonne
La Roche sur Ion
39
Poitou
40
Luçon
Fontenay
Pertuis Breton
I. d'Oléron
La Rochelle
Niort
Pertuis d'Antioche
Aunis
Rochefort
55
St. Jean
Ile de Ré
Le Château
La Tremblade
Saintes

REFERENCE TO DÉPARTEMENTS

1 Nord	45 Jura
2 Pas de Calais	46 Doubs
3 Seine Inférieure	47 Haute Savoie
4 Somme	48 Ain
5 Oise	49 Rhône
6 Aisne	50 Loire
7 Ardennes	51 Puy de Dôme
8 Meurthe et Moselle	52 Creuse
9 Meuse	53 Haute-Vienne
10 Marne	54 Charente
11 Seine-et-Marne	55 Charente Infér.
12 Seine	56 Gironde
13 Seine et Oise	57 Dordogne
14 Eure	58 Corrèze

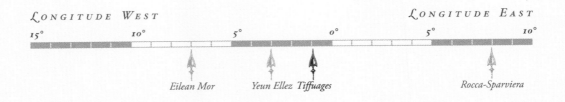
47° N – 1°06′ W

TIFFAUGES

CASTLE OF A KILLER

Tiffauges was one of the homes of Gilles de Rais, the Baron de Retz, who is infamous for the 140 murders he has said to have committed of young people of both sexes aged between eight and eighteen; to say nothing of an undeniable talent for swindling his immediate family and other relatives, resorting to violence where necessary. Although not the only scene of his atrocious crimes—he is also accused of carrying out assassinations, committing acts of physical abuse, and hiding the remains of his victims in his other châteaux of Machecoul and Champtocé-sur-Loire—Tiffauges occupies a highly symbolic place in this macabre litany. This is no doubt due to the interest taken in it by the young man of noble—and very wealthy—lineage who devoted himself to developing the "residential" part of this austere fortress in the Vendée, built three centuries earlier. The castle had come into his possession through his wife, Catherine de Thouars, whom he married in 1420 at the tender age of sixteen, as part of the attractive dowry she brought with her.

Their marriage had not been without obstacles. Not only had it been vetoed by the Church on the basis of the consanguinity of the future spouses, it was also opposed by both branches of the family, who were then at daggers drawn, leaving Gilles no option but to kidnap his quasi-betrothed in order to force everyone's hand. It should also be pointed out that this was not the first matrimonial difficulty he had experienced, having already been betrothed to other heiresses at the age of twelve and then fifteen. To make sure he was getting his conjugal life off to a good start, Gilles de Rais then had his mother-in-law abducted and locked up in order to persuade her to hand over a number of her properties.

The impetuous lord of Tiffauges went on to earn a fine reputation for himself, first in the service of King Charles VII, and subsequently fighting the English as a comrade-in-arms of Joan of Arc, for which he was rewarded with the title of Marshall of France in 1429. The higher you rise, the harder you fall, as they say. . . . What really happened behind the fortified walls at Tiffauges? Some testified Gilles de Rais tried to summon a demon there. Clearly the court in Nantes was sufficiently convinced by the testimony of the accused's servants, the bones discovered in his châteaux, and his own confessions (obtained, it should be said, without torture, as his noble status spared him this inconvenience) to condemn him to death and send him to the gallows in October 1440.

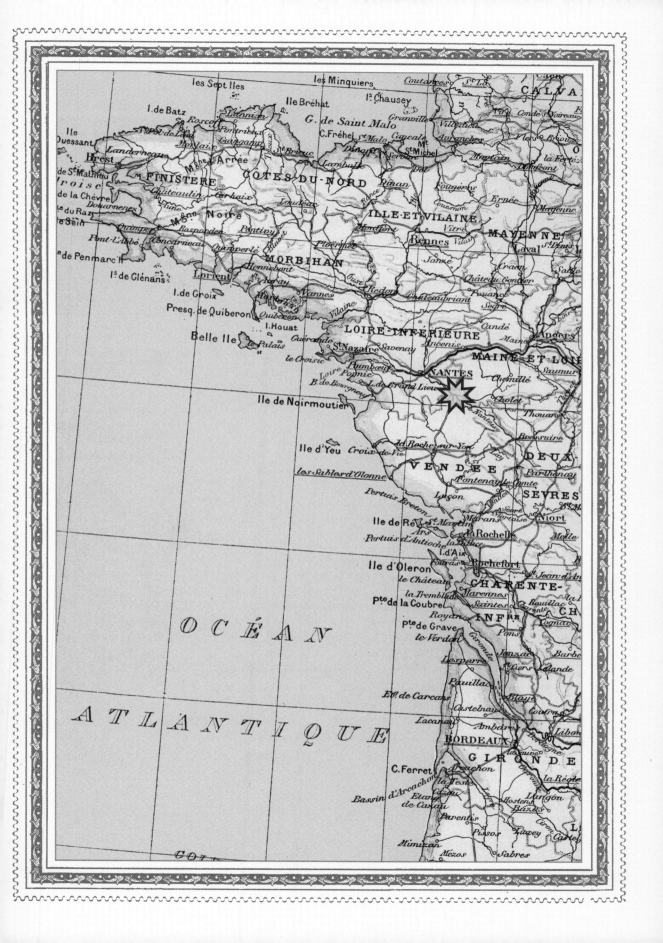